THE ISLANDS SERIES

THE ARAN ISLANDS

THE ISLANDS SERIES

* Published in the United States by Stackpole
† Published in the United States by David & Charles
  Distributed in Australia by Wren Publishing Pty Ltd, Melbourne

THE ARAN ISLANDS

by *DAPHNE D. C. POCHIN MOULD*

DAVID & CHARLES

NEWTON ABBOT

0 7153 5782 4

© Daphne D. C. Pochin Mould 1972

Set in eleven on thirteen point Baskerville
and printed in Great Britain by
Clarke Doble & Brendon Limited Plymouth
for David & Charles (Holdings) Limited
South Devon House Newton Abbot   Devon

CONTENTS

ILLUSTRATIONS

All photographs are by the author with the exceptions
shown above

MAPS

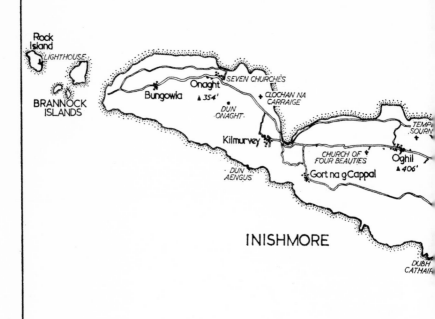

NORTH SOUND

Rock Island
LIGHTHOUSE

BRANNOCK ISLANDS

Bungowla

Onaght

▲ 354'

DUN ONAGHT

SEVEN CHURCHES

CLOCHAN NA CARRAIGE

TEMP SOURN

Kilmurvey

CHURCH OF FOUR BEAUTIES

Oghil

▲ 406'

DUN AENGUS

Gort na gCappal

INISHMORE

DUBH CATHAIR

N

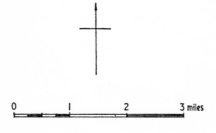

0   1   2   3 miles

ARAN ISLANDS
County Galway

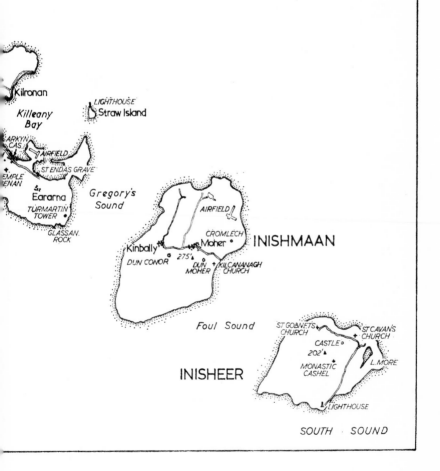

Kilronan

Killeany
Bay

LIGHTHOUSE
Straw Island

ARKYN
CAS

AIRFIELD

ST ENDAS GRAVE

TEMPLE
ENAN

Eararna

Gregory's
Sound

TURMARTIN
TOWER

GLASSAN.
ROCK

AIRFIELD

CROMLECH

Moher

INISHMAAN

Kinbally

275'

DUN CONOR

DUN
MOHER

KILCANANAGH
CHURCH

Foul Sound

ST GOBNETS
CHURCH

ST CAVAN'S
CHURCH

CASTLE
202'

L.MORE

INISHEER

MONASTIC
CASHEL

LIGHTHOUSE

SOUTH · SOUND

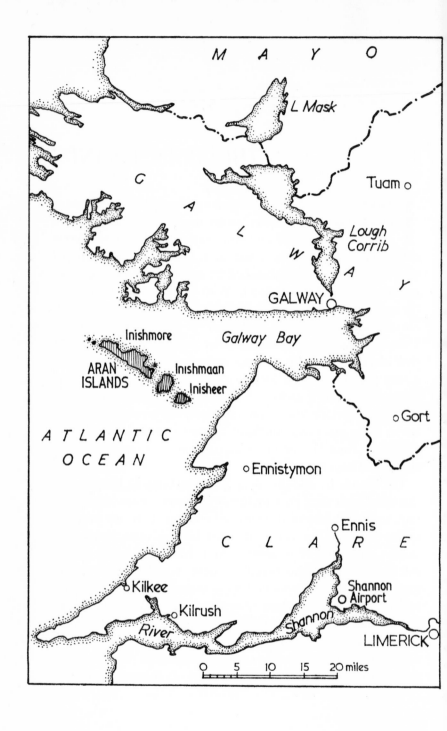

1 THE ARAN ISLANDS

F
ROM the air the Aran Islands appear as three grey slabs of rock, like a breakwater across the entry to Galway Bay. They are patterned with little stone-walled fields, with great cliffs fronting the Atlantic, white sandy beaches on the landward side, and clusters of whitewashed houses, some slated, some still retaining the traditional thatch. With the possible exception of the now deserted Blasket islands in county Kerry, the Aran Islands are the best known and best loved of all offshore islands of Ireland. Their attraction and interest depend on many things : their island people, Irish speaking, and only recently emerged from a very primitive way of life; their beauty, bare rock, clear seas, bright flowers; their geology, a limestone *karst*, and its associated flora; their bird life; their Irish traditions. Nowhere else in Ireland are so many great monuments of the past crowded into so small a compass, from Megalithic chambered tomb to stone fort, ruined chapel and high cross.

The islands lie midway along the west coast of Ireland. Off that same coast there are a multitude of islands—some large, some tiny, some still inhabited, many more deserted. In the north in county Donegal lies Tory, still inhabited but often isolated by storms; and south of it, another Aran Island, on which people still live also. The Aran Islands of county Galway are, therefore, sometimes called the 'South Isles of Aran', especially by older writers, to distinguish them from the Donegal Aran. There are more islands off the coast of Mayo, and Galway, north of the Aran Islands : Achill and Clare, Inishturk, Inishshark, Inishboffin, to name only some of the larger and still inhabited ones. South of the Aran Islands, there is a gap in the line of offshore islands until

11

the mouth of the Shannon is reached; then comes county Kerry, with the Magharees, the Blaskets, and turning east along the south coast of the country, another multitude of islets in counties Kerry and Cork. Nearly all these islands attracted early settlers and have the remains of Celtic monasteries and hermitages, as well as more recent deserted farms.

The Aran Islands then, lie across the mouth of Galway Bay, elongated north-west to south-east, and Irish tradition would make them the last remnant of a land barrier that enclosed a lake that later, when the sea broke through, became Galway Bay. The Aran Islands, to be exact, lie between latitudes 53° 2′ and 53° 9′ and longitudes 9° 30′ and 9° 51′. The northernmost island is the largest, and accordingly named Inishmore, in Irish *Inis Mor*, Great or Big Island. It is about 8 miles long by 2 across, and comprises 7,635 acres. Between it and Inisheer, is Inishmaan, *Inis Meain*, Middle Island. Inisheer, the south-easternmost of the three, is East Island, with various spellings in Irish, of which the most correct seems to be *Inis Oirr*. These two islands are smaller and rounder than the elongated Inishmore and lack its very high sea cliffs. Inishmaan is about 3 miles by 2, and of 2,252 acres; and Inisheer about 2 miles square, of 1,400 acres.

To the north the islands reach out toward Connemara and county Galway, and to the south to county Clare, the limestone hills of the Burren and the high cliffs of Moher. Inisheer has strong links with county Clare, from which it is separated by some 5 miles of sea; Inishmore is orientated rather toward Connemara, whose nearest point, the offshore islands of Gorumma and Lettermore, is 6 miles away. But Galway city, the main port for the islands, is some 30 miles away at the head of the bay.

To the west of the Aran Islands is the open Atlantic, no land until the New World is reached, and accordingly the great seas which pound the Aran cliffs and sometimes drive spray right across the islands have built up enormous force out in the ocean. Twice at least the islands have been the landfall for first transatlantic crossings, let alone the visit of Columbus to Galway, when he must have sailed past Aran. In 1919, just north of the islands, in Connemara near Clifden, Alcock and Brown landed, after the first successful transatlantic flight. In 1966, John Ridgway and Chay Blyth came into Kilronan on Inishmore, after making the first crossing by rowing boat.

Because of their setting, the islands are always aware of the sea, and it is often rough, both on the passage to Galway up the bay and in the narrow sounds between the islands. The North Sound separates Inishmore from Connemara and county Galway; the South Sound Inisheer from county Clare; Gregory's Sound, about 1 mile across at its narrowest, lies between Inishmore and Inishmaan; and Foul Sound, which is $1\frac{1}{2}$ miles at the narrowest, between Inishmaan and Inisheer. There are also old Irish names for these sounds, which are called *bealach*, the same word that is applied to a pass through the hills. North Sound is Bealach Lougha Lurgan—after Lough Lurgan, the fabled lake supposed to have occupied what now is Galway Bay. Gregory's Sound is also named Bealach na h-Aite, from a neighbouring rise of land on Inishmore known as Aite. Foul Sound is Bealach na Fearbhach, from a district of Inishmaan called Fearbhach; and South Sound is Bealach na Finnis, from the Finnis rock off Inisheer, a place of many shipwrecks.

Geologically and botanically the Aran Islands belong to county Clare and the Burren district, of which they are an extension. Politically they are in county Galway, but ecclesiastically included in the diocese of Tuam, not Galway. Their people are physically rather a race apart—it is usually easy to spot an Aran man among a mainland crowd—and Irish is their first language. There are no other islands, no other place, in Ireland, at all like Aran, and the stranger is likely to be more struck, perhaps inclined to over-stress, the islands' otherness, their difference from the rest of Ireland, than their growing likeness to it in way of life and similarity of economic difficulties.

Under 2,000 people now live on the islands. Inishmore has about 900, and the two smaller islands about 320 each. In summer the population rises dramatically as visitors crowd in, not only from Ireland but from all over the world, and the numbers are further increased by summer schools where mainland children come to improve their knowledge of Irish.

Most islanders are bilingual, with fluent English, but Inishmaan, the most isolated of the three islands, still has (as of 1972) a number who only speak Irish, even if they probably follow a certain amount of English. Island Irish is spoken well and clearly, and it is a good place for students of the language to go. Many, in fact, do come to Aran.

The stranger can reach the islands in a variety of ways—by the regular mailboat from Galway; by other shipping, such as curragh or fishing boat, from the coasts of Clare or Connemara; or by his own boat. Since 1970 there has also been a regular air service by a ten-seater 'Islander' twin, flying from Galway and the international airport of Shannon to Killeany airfield, Inishmore, and, from 1973, to Inishmaan also. The owner of a light plane can fly in to the new Aran airstrips, undoubtedly the most interesting in Ireland.

The stranger arriving by boat is probably more struck by the unusual character of island life than the one who comes by plane, but the latter gets a far better impression of the islands, From the air the great cliffs which edge Inishmore, reaching a maximum height of some 300ft; the bare limestone plateau; the great stone forts; the settlement pattern of village and stone-walled fields; are seen in a way impossible from any vantage point on land or sea. But it is better to visit the lesser islands by mailboat, for then the curraghs, the canvas-covered successors of prehistoric skin-covered craft, are rowed out to meet her, since neither Inisheer nor Inishmaan has a pier. These curraghs carry all the islanders' imports and exports, including passengers. If it is the time for the cattle sales, the cattle are swum out behind curraghs and winched aboard the mailboat. The men who row the curraghs very often come out in traditional homespun suits, with sleeveless waistcoats of a blue-flecked grey tweed; and, while most now wear rubber seamen's boots, some still sport the homemade shoe of rawhide cowskin called a pampootie.

The mailboat can tie up on Inishmore, and on that island, which now has an efficient fishing fleet of small trawlers and lobster boats, the number of curraghs is decreasing. Here the visitor is met by pony and trap, with the suggestion of a sightseeing tour, but islanders themselves get around on Inishmore by car and motorcycle as well as in horsedrawn vehicles. To the English speaker the process of landing on the smaller islands is immediately slightly foreign, with Irish the normal language of communication, and Irish in quickfire shouting as the ship's manifest is checked, and the goods—bottled gas, building material, potato crisps, fertiliser—handed into the bobbing curraghs.

It is difficult to believe that this area is part of the same country as the green lanes and fields of county Limerick and county Clare round Shannon airport. Bare rock, hot to the hand in summer sun, gleaming silver in rain, is everywhere. On the fields, or in the cracks of the limestone pavements, all through spring and summer, wildflowers riot in many colours. More especially the person who comes by small boat or little plane is aware of the great silence. Switch off the engine and there are none of the sounds of modern living.

The islands are still very quiet places, with cuckoos and larks singing, corncrakes rasping in the hayfields, and the occasional quiet purr of the regular Aer Arann aircraft. In storm it is different, for then the thunder of the seas is everywhere—you can walk on the east side of the island and still hear the waves breaking on the western cliffs.

In wintertime the islands are dark places, for there is no street lighting, and nothing to compete with the brightness of the stars overhead or the clear moonlight. A moonless clouded winter night is very black indeed, though 30 miles away, if it is clear, are the brilliant seafront lights of Galway town and the resort of Salthill.

They are islands of an immense clarity of light, where open sea and sky and the bare rock combine to produce a kind of luminosity in the air. In clear weather the view from their low heights (the highest point, on Inishmore, is only 406ft above sea level) is vast. To the south the mountains of Kerry appear as a

15

low line on the horizon—some 65 miles distant. The nearer Cliffs of Moher in county Clare and the white limestone heights of the Burren stand out, sharp in every detail, in certain lights. Northward are the quartzite heights of the Twelve Bens and the ridge of the Maamturks, the mountain groups of Connemara, and offshore the many islets north of Aran. There are ever-changing patterns of light and cloud formation over these distant views and over the expanse of the sea; the islands have very much their own climate, and it is common for them to be parched in sunshine while showers, and heavy downpours, can be watched on all the neighbouring hills.

Aran people have been, until recently, subsistence farmer-fishermen. Today Inishmore's young fishermen have been making good catches, and good money, from modern boats; the little farms still rear young cattle on the limestone pastures that fetch very good prices from mainland buyers. Farming, however, is hardly a livelihood on these tiny plots in modern times, though fishing is; and tourism, with the growth of guest houses as well as of homes taking one or more visitors, is of vital importance to island economy. Like all western areas of Ireland, there has been and still is much emigration even if only to civil-service jobs in Dublin, and these emigrants have a long tradition of sending back part of their earnings to keep the old home going. For the Irish Government, committed to Irish as the national language and to the prosperity of the western districts, it should be important that Aran should survive.

Living on islands today is difficult, with the added cost of transport on everything that must be brought in or taken out. The attraction of the mainland has increased, with consequent emigration and often the ultimate abandonment of the island. The Aran Islands appear big enough and potentially prosperous enough to escape this final stage, but they still need more outlets for the skill and intelligence of their people, especially the girls, at home. As it is, the majority of island youngsters will not only receive their secondary education on the mainland, but look for jobs there also. In the winter months, apart from Christmas, when

Page 17 (above) Central Inishmore. This picture is of the highest ground in the three islands. It shows the great ring fort of Dun Oghil, and alongside, nearer the camera, the remains of the first lighthouse to be erected on the islands. It shows also the typical pattern of Aran fields, with rain water cisterns in them. This is also the area of the old town, Baile na Sean, whose rath and beehive huts were mapped by G. H. Kinahan in the 1860s. However, few traces now seem to show up from the air, at least on this portion of the complex of old ruins; (below) Ring fort, Dun Conor, Inishmaan. Probably the finest of its type in Ireland. The old monastic site with St Kennerg's grave lies immediately right of the (1939) island church. Thatched house with bush in front, third left from church, is where J. M. Synge stayed

Page 18 (above) Clochan na Carraige, Inishmore. This very fine example of a beehive hut, built without mortar, is of local limestone but with glacial erratics standing out, a white rounded boulder among them. Many more such huts are now ruined or totally destroyed on the islands; (below) Dun Aengus, Inishmore, central citadel with outer walls and *chevaux de frise* of standing stones for extra defence round second, outer wall. Buttresses supporting inner wall were put up during Board of Works restoration

everyone who can comes home, any gathering of Aran people—
for instance at Sunday Mass—consists mainly of the elderly and
children up to secondary school starting age, with few young and
young middle-aged people in the group.

Present difficulties of living on offshore Irish islands are in complete contrast with their more remote past, when the places were
in fact often more attractive to settlers than the mainland. And
in the early centuries of Irish history, the Aran Islands were
neither outposts nor remote, but very much in the centre of Irish
communication lines and settlement.

Ancient Ireland was a heavily wooded country with vast expanses
of undrained bogland as well; and both forest and bog made travel
and agriculture difficult. The eskers, or dry ridges of sand and
gravel laid down probably by streams flowing under the Ice Age
glacier sheets, formed some easy routes across the bogs, and the
greatest of these, the Esker Riada, ran west from the Dublin/
Tara area on the east coast to Galway on the west. Travel by
small boat was easy by comparison with much land travel, and
there was a great deal of island and coastal sailing along the west
of Ireland. The Aran Islands lay just where this north to south
sea route met the east to west Esker Riada, that is at the junction
of the sea and land routes, and their light soil, easily worked, and
sandy beaches on which small craft could be easily run ashore,
were extremely attractive to early and subsequent settlers.

The Megalithic (Great Stone) people who built the great
chambered cairns of Newgrange and Knowth in Ireland and the
stone circles, of which Stonehenge in England is the most famous,
arrived in Ireland some 3,000 years before the birth of Christ or
even earlier. They settled on the Aran Islands, among other places
in Ireland, and some of their ruined tombs still remain. Later
came the construction of the great stone 'forts' for which the
islands are so well known and of which Dun Aengus is the most
famous—perhaps in pre-Christian or, more probably, in early
Christian times.

With the coming of Christianity to Ireland in the early fifth
century, and the development of monasticism in the sixth, many

B

19

large monasteries were established on the larger offshore islands and hermitages on the smaller ones. 'Aran of the Saints', as the islands are sometimes called, played a key role in this early Christian history, for St Enda's monastery at Killeany on Inishmore was one of the first great Irish monasteries, a pioneering establishment to which a whole litany of Irish saints and monks came to study and observe, before going on to make their own foundations elsewhere. If the Seven Romans stone at Onaght on Inishmore refers to foreigners who died and were buried on the islands, there must have been visitors from abroad as well as from mainland Ireland. It is known that foreign pilgrims and students came in some numbers in the early Christian centuries to Irish monasteries and centres of learning, and it is probable that they would have come to Aran as well as to other places. In the transport of those days it would be as easy to come to Aran as to Clonmacnois on the Shannon, and Clonmacnois received, it is said, boatloads of foreign pilgrims and students.

In the fourteenth century a Franciscan friary was founded on Inishmore, at Killeany, close to St Enda's old monastery. In the secular world at the same time the islands were held by the family of O'Brien of county Clare, who had an agreement with Galway to protect the shipping lanes to that city from pirate attacks. Who controls Aran, controls the sea roads to Galway.

So in Elizabethan times, Aran and Inishboffin became the key points of the whole western coastal defence. Inishboffin lies north of Aran, off the Connemara coast, a very different place geologically and scenically from Aran, but the two were worked as parts of one garrison. All through the seventeenth century, Arkyn Castle, which is also at Killeany, was subjected to attacks, rebuildings, and enlargements, and a military garrison was maintained there. Cromwell's men found the old churches—St Enda's at Killeany and the Franciscan church—ready cut quarries for enlarging Arkyn.

If one recalls that Prince Charles Edward made his landfall on lonely Eriskay in the Scottish Hebrides in 1745, the concern of the central government for guarding the western coasts, which with populations often friendly to an invader were a long weak link in their defences, is very understandable. It was not until early in the eighteenth century that Aran ceased to be of strategic importance, and the islands passed into that remote existence of subsistence farming and fishing that so enchanted visitors like J. M. Synge and startled cinema audiences as Aran men took their frail looking curraghs into mountainous seas in Robert Flaherty's classic documentary, *Man of Aran*.

An absentee landlord rejoiced in the title 'Earl of Aran' and collected a very large amount, for such country, in rent; but for the islanders life was bare subsistence. If J. M. Synge was delighted to record how everything was homemade, the first district nurse, not long after Synge's book appeared (1907), could record that on Inishmaan, Synge's favourite island, 'most of the people are improperly nourished'. Her account, published in 1917, tells of how much (and also how little) a district nurse could do alone when faced with cases like that of a little girl on Inisheer, 'seriously ill suffering from the effects of malnutrition and beyond all hope of recovery'.

Conditions on the islands today are very different, and nobody is anywhere near starvation level. Yet the present standard of living and amenities, which would have seemed extreme luxury to the islanders of Synge's time and his play *Riders to the Sea*, are not good enough to prevent emigration.

The young islander today has the education, means and opportunities were unknown to earlier generations, though many did take the emigrant ship for America. If the islands fail to offer similar opportunities, they are bound to lose their young men and women.

With the coming of the air service, bringing the international airport of Shannon, with jet connections to all parts of the world, within twenty minutes' flying time, the islanders have experienced a great psychological change. Even if one does not want to fly, the service is there; the aircraft can operate when the seas are too rough for the ship, and the feeling of being confined on an island is gone.

The outside world rediscovered the Aran Islands in the nineteenth century, though the first detailed account, a vivid pen picture, was written by Roderick O'Flaherty back in 1684 (see Appendix F). Antiquarians, botanists, and ornithologists reported on the islands, and the Ethnological Section of the British Association visited them in 1859. The physical characteristics, customs and way of life of the inhabitants were recorded in some detail by these early visitors. For playwright J. M. Synge, the Aranman was rather in the nature of the 'Noble Savage', free and self-sufficient, steeped in Gaelic tradition and speaking the Irish language to perfection. Synge's *The Aran Islands* (1907) records first-hand just how life was lived at the turn of the century, and his excellent photographs show what it looked like. He is a very important witness to island life as it once was lived.

The early visitors had to make their own travel arrangements. John O'Donovan, working on the first Ordnance Survey of Ireland in 1839, arrived in a boat from Galway's fishing village of Claddagh called the *Mountain Maid*, and it cost the Survey party 18s. Only in 1891 was a regular steamboat service initiated, from Galway, with the paddle-steamer *Citie of the Tribes* (an old title for Galway city).

John O'Donovan's *Ordnance Survey Letters* record the extent and condition of the Aran Island monuments, stone forts, chapels and inscribed crosses. Their proper conservation later became an issue, and an urgent one, for they were handy quarries for new building of house or field wall. The chapels were still places of pilgrimage on their respective saints' days, and likely to be left alone, but the stone forts were protected by no such feeling of history or holiness.

The Board of Public Works took charge of the principal island monuments in 1880, but took no immediate action for their preservation until the Rev James Graves sent them a strongly worded appeal in 1883. He said that the Board must at once intervene to halt 'the injuries inflicted on, and impending total destruction of' the stone forts, clochans (beehive drystone cells) and churches. The Board replied that it was not aware of any urgency

in the matter but would look into it. It then undertook such conservation work as that period knew it, repairing and restoring the
remains. Archaeology was then a very young science, and the kind
of recording before 'restoration' that would now take place was
unknown. The Board's instructions were much more in the
nature of sending a team of local men to 'mend the wall' as best
they knew how, and, naturally, there was some destruction of
original features and alteration of original plans. O'Donovan and
some other pre-1880 antiquarians have left accounts of the monuments which indicate to a certain extent how much the 'restoration' changed them. If the work had not been done, however,
they would in all probability have been largely destroyed, and
the modern visitor, while deploring the loss of certain authentic
ancient detail, must rejoice that the work was taken in hand in
time to preserve the sheer magnificence of the great stone forts.

The first organised effort to improve the quality of island life
was made by the Congested Districts Board, which was reporting
on conditions in all the western districts of Ireland at about the
same time that the Board of Works was repairing the Aran forts.
But conditions only very slowly altered for the better. The Aran
people themselves look back to two landmarks—Irish independ-
ence, when the Free State was set up (1921), and then the granting
of the dole, public assistance, to a number of islanders, which
helped raise their living standards above the previous subsistence
level.

It is, in fact, a paradox of modern times that while today the
Aran Islanders enjoy the highest standard of living they have ever
known, their future is also probably more doubtful than at any
other period. Their problem is to find enough varied and profitable outlets for their people on the islands themselves to keep
sufficient men and women at home to maintain full island community life.

2   A WORLD OF STONES

THE Aran islands are, as already remarked, a limestone
karst, a gently tilted plateau consisting mainly of bare
rock. Of their total area of 18 sq miles, only about 6 are
cultivated, the rest being rough grazing of sorts and bare rock
pavements deeply fissured with joints. It is, then, a world of rock
—a small intimate world full of intriguing variations. Because
there is nothing larger to scale it by, each island tends to appear
larger than it is, and distances look longer until one actually
walks them.

GEOLOGY

The rock of the islands is a continuation of that which builds the
bare limestone hills of the Burren in Clare, in clear view of the
islands on a fine day. The bulk of the rock is a massive grey
Carboniferous limestone, which dips very gently to the south-south-
west. Interbedded with the limestone are thinner bands of cal-
careous shale. The differential weathering of the two rock types
has resulted in marked steps where they meet, so that the islands
rise in a series of terraces. It is along these terraces, sheltered from
the wind by the cliffs behind them, that men have built their
homes and made their arable fields; and when a road system was
developed, it took its natural line along them.

The Aran limestones differ from those of the Burren in having
more shale in the series and more shaly particles in the actual
limestone, which makes it less suitable for building stone. However, the Rev Kilbride, Church of Ireland pastor on Inishmore
and a noted early antiquarian, informed the first geological sur-

24

veyors about 1870 that, when the lighthouse was building, stone from the south-west quarry near Tonefechney was taken to Dublin to be worked as a marble. There are in the limestones some dolomitised zones but no trace of mineralisation has been reported. To anyone walking and scrambling over the Aran limestones, the fossils are an obvious feature. There are marked layers of shells, with many remains and often the broken fragments of crinoids, the so-called 'sea lilies', in some abundance. The geological survey for water made on Inishmaan in 1971 noted traces of some burrowing worm, or other marine animal, in the rather muddy limestone close to some of the shale strata.

In the same survey some study was made of the fossils, and for the technically minded this suggested that the top of the succession on this island was about 30m below the base of the Namurian sub-division of the Carboniferous. Throughout the series the survey noted *Gigantoproductus, Chaetetes, Oibuno-phyllum* and *Lithostrotion (Paneiradiale* and *Junceum* groups). In one shell bed, *Cyrtina septosa* was possibly identified and abundant—this was above shale band No 5. *Lonsdaleia* and *Palaeozimilia regia* were collected from loose blocks of rock lying on the top of the final 10m of the island succession. No other detailed study of the islands' rocks and fossils has yet been made, the initial Geological Survey, published in 1871, being, naturally, a brief outline only.

The limestone is strongly jointed, and this joint system controls the development of the great cliffs of Inishmore. These rise to a maximum height of 300ft; at Dun Aengus the drop to the sea below is 265ft. The cliffs are clean cut, sheer, not very suitable as nesting places for bird colonies, as the faces lack a system of ledges, but allowing the islanders to fish, with very long weighted lines, from the high cliff tops.

Inland, the joints are enlarged by rainfall run-off dissolving the limestone, as it percolates downwards. So the landscape is one of bare rock criss-crossed by deep and steep-sided fissures, in which grow numerous ferns and dwarf bushes. In some places along the shore, as, for instance, at the head of the strand in Kilronan Bay, the rock is etched into fantastic shapes by seawater solution action. At certain places along the cliffs there are puffing holes— the inshore part of the roof of a sea cave has fallen in so that the waves, driven into the cave's mouth, spout through the hole at its head in geyser-like fashion. With a rough sea running, these puffing holes can send the spray mounting to a considerable height and are well worth watching at such times. There are fine examples to be found on the western shore of Inishmaan, where they are formed in the wave-cut limestone terraces between the normal high-tide line and the great storm beach.

In the summer of 1971 the Sub Aqua Club of Queen's University, Belfast, made a descent of the famous hole of the serpent near Dun Aengus, and swam out to the open sea, with much enjoyment in the exceptionally clear water.

As in all limestone country, there are no rivers, nor indeed much room for them, in the little islands, though there are a few streams. Springs are formed where the water seeping through the limestone meets the less pervious shale and moves out along its bedding planes, and there is, as one would expect, a relation between the good springs and people's houses. There are a few lakes, and behind Kilronan, a large *turlough*—a typical impermanent limestone country lake that fills with water in very wet periods but otherwise appears as a rather moist green flat.

Scattered about on the limestone pavements are large boulders of granite, with big pink feldspar crystals, and other rocks brought over when the Ice Age glaciers moved out from the mainland over the bay and islands. Sometimes the granite boulders are used to form base stones for island walls in a kind of regular pattern. At the old Celtic Church sites they are found to have been used as hollow *bullaun* stones—primitive mortars in which grain could be crushed by means of another stone, or shellfish de-shelled. As a harder rock, they are much more suitable for this purpose than the softer native limestones.

In addition to the various 'foreign' boulders carried to the islands by ice, the Geological Survey found some traces of boulder clay, suggesting that the islands had once had a much more complete clay cover. Additional confirmation comes from the fact that anyone wandering along the rocky fields of the islands, delighting in the lime-loving collection of wildflowers, may suddenly be surprised to find little patches of lime-hating heathers, both bell heather and ling (*Calluna vulgaris*). Although cropped close by animals, they appear to be growing reasonably well. Over in the Burren similar patches, and small areas of peat, have also been observed, the latter suggesting that once there was much more extensive peat cover. Add in the fact that a few trees still grow on Inishmore to a fair height, that the rock crevices and crag faces support a scrub growth of oak, hazel, blackthorn and whitethorn, among other species, and that there are vague but suggestive references to the islands once supporting more trees, and a new picture of their past emerges.

The general description of the Aran islands, fixed on film in *Man of Aran*, is of rock on which men have laboriously 'made' soil. However, it is perhaps not so much a making as a remaking of land. The traces of boulder clay, of heathery peat cover, and of woodland suggest that the islands originally had soil suitable for scrub at least, and that man by over-grazing, careless cultivation, cutting of trees for fire and building may have laid Aran bare and then tried to redress the balance by laboriously 'making' soil.

Certainly the Burren seems to have lost soil and trees in historic times. Flying over it one sees a network of very old fields and stone *raths* (ring forts, the fortified homesteads of the farmers who owned the old fields), and these fields run right over the high and now bare Burren ridges, well above the present levels of farm settlement. The workable land-level has dropped, not merely, as in many hilly regions in Ireland, because the intense land hunger —an overcrowded district seeking another potato plot—has eased off, but because erosion has increased at the higher altitudes. On the Aran Islands also it seems likely that serious soil erosion took place during historic times, coupled possibly with some climatic change.

The Aran Islanders 'made' many of their fields on the bare rock. The fissures in the rock were filled in with broken stones, and the surface pavement broken up to give a 'key' to retain the seaweed, sand and soil then spread over it. The seaweed and sand were carried up in homemade creels on donkey or human back; the soil, sometimes scraped from the fissures in the rock pavements, where it collects, was spread on top to complete the job. Pat Mullen, writing in 1934 (*Man of Aran*), recalls a neighbour whose need for soil was so desperate that he would willingly pull down and rebuild his boundary walls in order to gather the clay that had accumulated under the stones. This represented a great deal of heavy work for very little, as Aran field walls are constructed, in drystone, of large and small stones gathered off the fields they enclose, and are anything from 4 to 7 ft high. Many island fields have been 'made' by this method. It is still done when the need arises, and, indeed, provides a means whereby the islanders could still add quite an amount of extra arable land to their holdings.

However, along the low strands fronting Galway Bay there are extensive sand dunes and sandy areas, and a good depth of soil in the little fields behind them. Vegetables flourish in such ground, and experimental plots to produce tulip bulbs did very well on Inishmaan a few years ago.

In these areas, especially on Inisheer, there is a good deal of bare sand and the dunes shift in the sandstorms produced by high winds. On Inisheer an attempt has been made to anchor the sand by planting rectangular beds of marram grass. The power of wind-driven sand can be well demonstrated on this island at the old church of St Cavan, which is engulfed by a large sandhill, and only kept in sight by diligent and regular excavation. The old church gables only just top the surrounding sand and it stands in a deep artificial hole in the dune. Round about, the stone walls of old fields appear and disappear through the sand as it shifts. On Inishmore a whole series of clochans (beehive drystone huts) and what appears to have been part of a Megalithic tomb were revealed by a storm of the 1860s that shifted the sand cover off them. This latter site is on the eastern tip of the island, the district called Eararna.

In fact, one can encounter a real sandstorm in a high wind on these sandy areas of the islands.

Wind, blown sand and blown sea spray, and summer drought are all part of the Aran Islands scene. Writing in 1887, Oliver J. Burke noted : 'The meteorological aspirations of the Aran peasant are for rain, diametrically the opposite of what their brethren on the mainland desire'.

Aran weather, influenced like all the west coast of Ireland by the Gulf Stream, is mild, without frost or snow. If snow does fall, it melts immediately. Fog is rare but an overcast of low stratus cloud common. But it is seldom that the cloud comes low enough to cover the highest point of the islands, Dun Oghil (406ft).

Even a brief stay on the islands will convince the visitor that they have their own climate, but unfortunately, up to the present time, no proper meteorological recording station has been established, so the full extent of their peculiarities is not exactly known. Rainfall, however, was recorded over a longish period of years at Kilronan, Inishmore, and these records show that it is less than that on the adjacent mainland. In the period from 1931 to 1960 the average annual rainfall at Kilronan was 1,128mm a year. This compares with average yearly falls along the north-west, west and south-west coasts of from 1,125mm to 1,500mm. Shannon airport, though, on the plain of county Clare, has less rain than Aran, averaging 930mm per annum over the period 1931 to 1960. Shannon is about 40 miles from the islands. Very much heavier falls occur regularly on the Connemara mountains north-east of Aran. The long fiord, the only fiord in Ireland, of Killary Harbour, is a trifle closer than Shannon, and the rainfall recorded at Aasleagh at its head, among the hills, reaches about 2,413mm a year. These heavy falls on the mountains may actually be seen from the Aran Islands, where there is much lower precipitation and often actual drought.

29

THE ARAN ISLANDS

The monthly averages for Kilronan in the period 1931 to 1960 are as follows:

Jan	Feb	Mar	Apr	May	Jun	Jul	Aug	Sept	Oct	Nov	Dec
116	77	72	56	61	75	106	94	106	116	116	133

mm

Thus December is normally the wettest month and April the driest, as they often are over the rest of Ireland.

The bare rock of the islands gives a curious lightness and opalescence to the scene even in dull weather, and this too is a feature from the air—a rare quality of colour and texture in the rocks below. The sea is clear of mud and, for the moment at least, of much refuse, and the air is clear likewise, with an immense outlook in fine weather to the coasts and hills of the mainland. The bare rock and light sandy soil dry out quickly, and the pastures turn brown early in summer. The dry summer of 1971 prevented, first, the early sowing, and then the proper growth of grass on the new airstrip of Inishmaan, so that this could not be brought into use that year as had been planned. Island cattle used frequently to be shipped over to the mainland for summer grazing—1955 was one year when this had to be done—and, when there were more horses on the islands than now, their transhipment, with all the trouble it involved, took place each summer to the pastures of Connemara.

When cement was introduced to the islands, the Inishmore farmers built water cisterns in nearly every field. These are large stone troughs with a sloping collecting shelf alongside, which catch and store the rainwater and reduce the labour, otherwise a daily chore, of carrying water to the animals in the fields. Of recent years, these cisterns have been built also on Inisheer and Inishmaan.

Shortage of water could be a critical factor in preventing the adoption of new projects in the islands. Inishmaan has enough at the moment for a piped supply to the existing houses, but it seems unlikely that it could take the additional strain of a large hotel, for example. Equally, new industries, if started on the islands, would require additional water supplies, which might be

30

difficult to provide. Off Iceland, the Westmann Islands, which also have a water problem, have solved it by laying a submarine pipe from the mainland, an expensive but original and effective solution.

The famous *Man of Aran* film, which stressed storm and wind, and thus wetness, hardly reflected the everyday realities of island life in dry spells. But the high winds and great seas come each year, especially in September and October. Forces 10 and 11 on the Beaufort scale are common at these periods. Force 10 has winds of 55–63 mph and is a whole gale; Force 11, with winds of 64–75 mph, is storm force. Such weather normally includes gusts of much greater velocity. The great seas are, of course, not solely due to local wind action, but may have built up right across the Atlantic, their wave size depending on their 'fetch'. High seas may be pounding the Aran shores while the local wind is relatively light, a fact important for the islands' air link, which often can fly when the mailboat cannot sail.

Wind-trimmed trees occur in some places, and in a really bad storm spray can fly right over the islands. These storms have cut the terrace platforms on the south-west of the islands, above normal tide lines, and behind them are piled the great boulders of the storm beaches, which the original Geological Survey aptly named the 'block beaches'. These storm beaches can be seen very well on Inishmore in the Glassan rock area—and on Inishmaan all along the west and south-west coastlines. On Inishmaan the storm beach climbs with the rise of the land, thinning as it goes to a lesser line of storm-flung boulders in the area where Synge used to look out over the sea, and where some rocks, built into a shelter, are known as Synge's Chair. The Inishmaan storm beach reaches a height of 170ft about sea level and is thought to be the highest in Ireland, a grim indication of what wave action can be like in these islands. Behind the immense pile of boulders of the Inishmaan storm beach are the stone walls enclosing the island fields, and, in very bad weather, these also have been broken and damaged by wave action.

Another striking example of what the sea can do is the wreck of the *Plassy* on Trawkeera Point in Inisheer. This ship belonged to the Limerick Steamship Company, and was wrecked on 8 March 1960, though all her crew were saved. She came in, stage by stage, and was finally cast up well above normal tide lines, to sit there, erect and as if still afloat—a curious sight from the sea, for she seems to be sailing out of the island.

Wave action causes cliff falls at intervals and sometimes an Aran fisherman, perched on a cliff top, has had a narrow escape when the rocks have collapsed. One man, at least, was lost in such a rock fall at Dun Aengus. When O'Donovan visited the islands in 1839, there had been a particularly bad storm on 7 January that had caused a good deal of damage to the remains of the headland fort of Dubh Cathair on Inishmore.

Rather different was the inundation of 1640 mentioned by Roderick O'Flaherty, when the sea swept across the low waist of Inishmore. The Geological Survey of 1871 thought this could have been a seismic tidal wave, for an earthquake was recorded that year. They also thought that the wave of 15 August 1852 might have had the same origin. This was a sudden monster wave that rose out of nowhere on a very fine day and swept away fifteen people who were fishing on the Glassan rocks in Inishmore, facing the sound to Inishmaan. Islanders said that it was a judgement on the men for fishing on a church holyday— the Assumption of the Mother of God.

FLORA

The islands are not only a world of stones, but also a world of flowers. The grey limestone sets off a brilliant procession of colour and variety from the gentians of spring to the russet bracken fronds of autumn. To walk the islands is to be continually delighted and surprised by their plants, bushes, and ferns.

Like the Burren, the Aran Island flora includes northern and alpine species, some of which probably established themselves as the Ice Age ended, mingled with southern varieties. The climate is mild, even if windy—the mean temperature estimated

for January is 6·5° C and for July 15° C—and there are primroses in flower at Christmas. There are a variety of different
environments for plant life : the deep damp clefts in the rock
pavements with their ferns, and the shallower crevices cushioned
at cliff side with sea pinks; the sand back from the strands with
sea holly and seakale; the rocks with samphire, bladder campion
and roseroot; the sandy fields and the less sandy ones; the
heathery spots on the higher, drier grassland; the dunes at
Killeany, with great pink bindweed blossom; and behind them
bright eggs and bacon, and tormentil that the islanders once used
for dye.

In spring there are saxifrages in flower on the rocks (*Saxifraga Sternbergii*, a form of cut-leaved saxifrage, and *S. hirta*),
and the brilliant spring gentians (*Gentiana verna*). Primroses and
cowslips, celandines and dandelions, in yellow and gold, are
abundant, and the violets are set off elegantly by the grey rocks,
just as the harebells are later in summer. The wind- and animal-
cropped cushions of hawthorn and blackthorn are covered with
white flowers, and later with berries; and the islanders claim the
island sloe to be sweeter than the mainland variety.

From the primrose and dandelion gold and the gentian blue
of early spring, the colour changes to a splendid purple red when
in the height of summer the bloody cranesbill (*Geranium sanguineum*) is in flower over all the pastures. Odd stray flowers of
this gaudy plant are still around even in October.

There are plants familiar from other lime pastures—the quak-
ing grass, the salad burnet and the bee orchid, together with
several other commoner orchids. There is bluegrass (*Sesleria*), the
hoary rockrose (*Helianthemum canum*), bushgrass (*Calamagrostis epigeios*), and quantities of wild garlic which flavour the milk
if the cows eat it. There is the little prickly sweet-scented white
Scots rose (*Rosa spinosissima*) as well as the ordinary dog rose.
Honeysuckle clambers over the stone walls. Beside them are the
tall spires of mullein (*Verbascum Thapsus*) and the pink bushy
mallow. Between the stones in June the wild strawberries ripen;
in autumn there are quantities of blackberries. The stonecrop

33

(*Sedum anglicum*) often grows on anthills and so has been given the local name of *poureen shingan,* 'ant house'. *Matthiola sinuata,* the sea stock, has been reported from Straw Island, but not since 1835. The arctic-alpine purple milkwort (*Astragalus danicus*) has spread to the sandy pastures from the limestone pavements; it is probably a survivor from glacial or early post-glacial times, and Inishmore and Inishmaan are its only Irish localities.

Maidenhair and hart's-tongue are among the ferns that flourish in the damp rock cracks and round the springs; and on the dry rock is the rich golden lichen, which, on Inishmaan, gives a glow to many of the island walls. At the time when O'Donovan was writing the *Ordnance Survey Letters* (1839), the islands exported samphire to Dublin. Below the tidemark there is carrageen moss, the seaweed used to make milk jellies.

The peculiar charm of the islands' flowers is in their setting of rock and pasture. Golden yellow bedstraw or white moon-daisy are equally set off by grey rock backgrounds; and the short grass, with wild thyme, knapweed, pink and yellow centaury, deep blue scabious, and plots of heather, is an invitation to search for more species.

The cliffs backing the terraced fields, and the walls themselves, often have heavy growths of ivy. In the clefts of the rocks and in moist sheltered places grow a number of dwarfed trees—oak, hazel, hawthorn, blackthorn, spindle, guelder rose, buckthorn and juniper. Kilronan and Kilmurvey still have trees of quite a reasonable size. O'Donovan, in 1839, thought the name Dun Oghil (*Dun Eochla*) meant an oak not, as often stated, a yew wood.

There are a number of early references to Aran woods. James Hardiman in his *History of Galway,* written in 1820, remarks of the islands that 'They were anciently overshadowed with wood, of which there are still very evident remains'. In a legal document of 20 June 1618 Henry Lynch of Galway assigned a moiety of the islands to William Anderson of Aran, excepting great trees, mines, minerals and hawks, though this exception is perhaps not more than a commonplace legal formula to limit what a tenant

Page 35 (left) St Cavan's church on Inisheer, nearly buried in the sand dunes. The O'Briens' castle in the background; *(right)* High cross fragments preserved in St Enda's Church, Killeany Inishmore. The horseman here has been compared with similar sculptures in the north-east of Scotland

Page 36 (above) Headland fort, Dubh Cathair, Inishmore. Beehive huts inside terraced defensive wall with *chevaux de frise* outside. Traces of much ruined huts can be seen on nose of headland. Note the undercutting of rocks by sea; *(below)* Kilronan Bay, Inishmore. Water-solution fretted limestone outcrops on the beach

could take from the land. Perhaps more to the point is the note of John O'Flaherty in a paper published in 1825 which says that fir, pine and oak wood were found in the island peat bottoms.

Messrs Haddon and Brown in their paper on the ethnology of the Aran Islands reported that early in the eighteenth century the last trees were situated at the Gort na Oonan quarter in Oghil townland. It was also said that the couples of the old houses at Gort na gCappul and Oatquarter were made from this wood. Oliver Burke, writing in 1887, quotes a letter giving information about the islands, written in 1886, which said that fifty years or so earlier a large part of Inishmore had trees, especially hazel, and that they reached a height of 20 to 26ft.

In 1951 Mrs Ganly of Kilronan, Inishmore, stated that her husband's grandmother's mother's grandmother remembered a calf being lost in the woods of Oghil. If Aran then, perhaps at the end of the eighteenth century, had woodland, it would most likely have been the low dense scrubby growth that still covers quite a part of the Burren, and in which it would be quite difficult to trail a straying calf.

FAUNA

Butterflies and moths in some variety flit over the island flowers, since Aranmen probably use less insecticide than many mainland farmers. Like many islands, Aran has its own peculiar creature, apparently a distinct species. It is a bumble bee, discovered in 1931 by C. Winckworth Allen, and so named after him *Bombus Smithianus allenellus*. The Aran bee differs from the normal *Bombus Smithianus* in that, as Stelfox describes it, 'the two basal segments of the abdomen [are] entirely, or almost entirely, clothed dorsally, as well as ventrally, with black hairs'. It lives in the sandy soil just above sea level in exposed places away from shelter or dense vegetation, its nest being made of closely woven shreds of grass.

It has already been mentioned that the Aran cliffs are too sheer to provide good nesting ledges for seabirds, but there are

c

a great many around for all that, including puffins and shags. Arctic terns nest on Inishmaan, and the fulmar petrel on Inishmore. The eider duck is a rare winter visitor to Galway waters, but barnacle geese no longer frequent the Brannock Islands.

Roderick O'Flaherty's account of the islands in 1684 speaks of their eyries of hawks, as well as of the colonies of red-legged Cornish choughs. The choughs are still there but the big birds of prey are unhappily gone from the whole district, islands and mainland alike. In 1841, as reported by William Thompson in his *Natural History of Ireland* (1849–50), the Golden eagle was not uncommon in Connemara and there were eyries in the Twelve Bens, and the Sea eagle was common. The Osprey was still about in the islands when Oliver Burke wrote in 1887, and he also reported the bittern on the low ground.

The Golden eagle seems to have bred in the Connemara mountains and in the Maamturks until the end of the 1880s, and the White Tailed eagle bred on the Mayo cliffs, to the north, until around 1898. Osprey and White Tailed eagle are now rare vagrants in the area. The Peregrine falcon survives and breeds in the islands.

The bird life of Aran varies somewhat from island to island. Thus the house sparrow is most abundant on Inishmaan, where there are the greatest number of thatched roofs for its nesting. R. F. Rutledge, who prepared a detailed list of the birds of counties Mayo and Galway in 1948, remarked that the swallow was plentiful on Inishmore, while only a few bred in cowsheds on Inisheer, and he had not seen it at all on Inishmaan. Occasionally unusual birds arrive, or kill themselves against the lighthouses. Eeragh light produced an Iceland Redwing (29 October 1930) and a Siberian chiffchaff (25 November 1943), for example. Rutledge saw an Arctic skua off Inisheer in June 1928.

In summer the corncrake rasps in island meadows, the cuckoo calls day and night, and larks sing. Larks and cuckoos appear to be much more numerous on the Aran Islands than elsewhere, unless it is merely that in the quiet they are more obvious. The cuckoo population was noted by William Thompson : 'Mr. R. Ball, remarked, when visiting the largest of the south isles of Aran, off Galway Bay, accompanied by the late lamented Dean of St. Patrick's, in June 1835, that cuckoos were particularly abundant there'. Thompson described the cormorants or shags of Aran, just as they still may be seen today.

> At Arranmore, off Galway Bay, Mr Ball and I, on the 8th of July 1834, saw a colony of cormorants at their breeding stations :— a tabular mass of limestone high above the sea, and from the summit of which a lofty range of precipice arose. The following day we saw twenty two of them swimming together in a close flock, between the two smaller islands.

Birds, in fact, are numerous on the islands and have exploited all the available types of habitat. Moorhens breed, evidently finding enough marshy ground for their liking. The bird population naturally varies with the time of year and migratory movements. A listing made in November 1957 included the whooper swan, the kestrel (flying over Inishmore), the black-throated and great-northern divers, tufted duck, heron, goosander, bar tailed godwit, redshank, greenshank, redwing, snow bunting and twite.

An otter was reported coming ashore on Inishmaan and fighting with and killing an island dog in 1971. Today this was regarded as very unusual by the islanders, though they say that twenty years ago otters were common.

Giraldus Cambrensis mentioned the Aran Islands, saying that 'though all Ireland abounds with rats, this island is free from any, for should that reptile be brought thither, it either leapeth into the sea, or being prevented, instantly dies'. James Hardiman in his *History of Galway* (1820) drily comments : 'This, however, is but one of the numerous fables and falsehoods with which that vain topographer amused his Oxford auditory respecting Ireland'.

The Aran Islands rabbits, isolated by the sea, escaped myxomatosis when that disease spread quickly over most of mainland Ireland. They find good cover in the island rocks, and in the walls, including those of the great forts.

Studies have been made of the non-marine mollusca—the land

39

snails and their kin—of the islands, and down on the strands, where the tides run favourably to cast them up, are piles of bright sea-snail shells and pink cowries. The rocky world of Aran, in fact, harbours a very considerable variety of plant and animal life.

3   THE GREAT STONE FORTS

NO date can be given for the coming of the first human settlers to Aran, nor indeed is it known who they were. In Northern Ireland there are coastal kitchen middens dating back to Mesolithic (Middle Stone Age) times, and they have been found in the Aran Islands in the dunes or in the soil. They consist of burned earth, limpet shells, fish bones, in typical refuse, but they could be of almost any age, and no research has been done as yet on them. Islanders in recent centuries as well as in Neolithic times have eaten limpets and dumped the shells in a heap behind the house. There is a very well defined midden layer in the dune section below St Cavan's church on Inisheer, and another (in the soil of the field) at the well preserved clochan on Inishmaan.

Blowing sand on Inisheer revealed the round site near the pier, now carefully preserved and marked, called Cnoc Raithnighe, which shows that the islands were occupied in the Bronze Age. In a storm in 1885 the sand was blown off the area, uncovering a circle and a low mound with urns and human bones. At a higher level were found upwards of twenty-four stone cists aligned east to west, and the suggestion has been made that this was a pagan burial place re-used during early Christian times. The urns are in the National Museum in Dublin, and the wall now enclosing the site was built by the Board of Works, c 1896.

There are several Megalithic stone tombs on the islands. These were built by the same people that built Stonehenge and the great chambered tombs of Newgrange, Knowth and Dowth on the River Boyne in Ireland, and may date back to 3000 BC. On the islands only the central chamber remains of the original burial mound or cairn which as on the Irish mainland, goes by the name of 'Dermot and Grania's Bed'. The tragic story of the elopement of Dermot (Diarmait) with Grania (Grainne) belongs to the Fionn cycle of ancient Irish stories; the lovers supposedly spent each night in a different place, which the storytellers finally located in the ruined Megalithic tombs of the countryside.

There is a well preserved Megalithic chamber on the heights of Inishmore, south of Cowrugh, looking across the island to Dun Aengus, but the 'Leaba Dhiarmada', north-east of Moher village on Inishmaan, has collapsed. T. J. Westropp, writing in 1895, speaks of the Inishmaan cromlech as still standing : 'two stones, 13ft 8in long and 4ft high, with a large block on top, the ends having been removed'. There was also a Megalithic cromlech at Kilmurvey on Inishmore and another was uncovered by blowing sand at Eararna, as already stated. Writing in 1938, T. H. Mason reported several other new sites from Inisheer—a cairn and a small passage grave north-west of the Post Office, and two small tumuli on the south-east of the island.

How many more early Megalithic tombs, stone forts and clochans have been rebuilt into walls and houses is anybody's guess. Aranmen, like all who live in stony lands, are handy at fitting rocks together, even enormous rocks, and the very modern and regular field walls in some areas, linked with the archaic styling of quite modern stone huts built for shelter or to store potatoes out in the fields, leaves one with the impression that for centuries men have been moving the stones of the islands from place to place. Subsidies for enclosing and reclaiming land, and for rainwater cisterns, have in recent years encouraged more shifting of the loose stonework.

Yet, for all that must have been destroyed, the Aran Islands remain famous for their great stone forts—Dun Aengus and Dubh Cathair (Doocaher), Dun Oghil and Dun Onaght, Dun Conor and the ancient rath around the O'Brien's castle on Inisheer. T. J. Westropp says there were the remains of ten stone forts on the islands in 1910, and from the air one can make out the ruins of some that are difficult to study at ground level because of the maze of island field walls. When John O'Donovan was in the islands (1839), the people told him that the strongest fort was at Oghil village, but only a portion of its huge stones remained, as the rest had been pulled apart to build houses.

The remaining great forts, by their sheer bulk and simple but impressive design, can almost overwhelm the stranger at a first sight, especially if he does not realise that they belong to a type of structure very common all over Ireland, and, moreover, that every rock built into their walls is one stone less on the small arable fields of Aran. From the air, for instance, it is very evident that the neat little fields circling Dun Conor on Inishmaan may owe a great deal to the volume of rock built into those fortress-like walls. Dun Conor, Dun Oghil, Dun Onaght and the Inisheer fort are all of the more or less circular type of rath found all over Ireland. Doocaher also belongs to the abundant headland fort series.

Dun Aengus, which is semicircular and backs on to the cliff edge, is much more unusual in design but not unique. As Westropp says, truly enough, it is 'one of the finest pre-historic forts of western Europe', and has inspired the most imaginative writing about the purpose of the island strongpoints. It is easy to picture men driven back ever westwards by successive early invasions of Ireland, and making a last stand between the devil of the enemy and the deep blue sea of the Atlantic. Thus R. A. S. MacAlister, writing on the archaeology of Ireland in 1939, said : 'Nothing but massacre, or drowning in the Atlantic deeps, awaited them outside their island fortresses : in desperation they heaped them up these vast walls, to shield them from the fury of the tempest that had burst upon their country and their kindred'.

It is easy to tie in this impression with the legendary account of the invasions of Ireland (and of course, there were successive settlements of the country by fresh waves of incomers). In the story of the invasions Aengus was a prince of the Fir Bolgs, the older conquered race, and it has been customary to identify the Aengus of Aran with him. T. F. O'Rahilly explored the invasion stories of Ireland very fully and thought the Laginian invasion took place in the third century BC. This would date the Aran forts, if Aengus and the Fir Bolgs erected them as they were thrust westward by the incomers.

One must immediately question whether the coming of new settlers and new cultures in early times to Ireland meant this kind of simple military operation and population shift—genocide in modern parlance. Almost certainly it did not. Ordinary people would not move, even if they got a new ruler, and quite certainly the Aran forts could not be held against sustained attack, for none of them have any water supply within their walls. But they would be excellent protection against the brief piratical raid to which any island might be exposed. To see them in their true context it is necessary to understand the whole ring-fort picture in Ireland. Dun Aengus may not even be prehistoric; it may be early Christian and its owner a wealthy farmer, not a gallant but defeated prince.

Ring forts, or to give them their folklore name 'fairy forts', are the commonest ancient monuments in Ireland. They are everywhere. T. J. Westropp went to the trouble of counting those marked on the Ordnance maps and the total reached 30,000. Many were missed by the early surveyors or are only visible from the air in low sun, or as crop marks or in newly ploughed soil. There could be 40,000 or more of them. Fewer than 100 of this multitude have been excavated.

They are generally circular structures, of single or multiple banks and ditches. The walls are of stone where this is available readily, of earth elsewhere. They are normally on good farming land, and, as may be seen best from the air, often in village-like groups or sprawling clusters, arranged in much the same way as modern Irish farmsteads. Inside the rings in stone-rich places like Aran remain the ruins of the owners' huts, in which they lived and worked; elsewhere the old huts can be traced by excavation and the finding of post holes. Often there is an underground passage or souterrain—some served as boltholes to the outside, but others remain within the fort and perhaps served to provide additional storage space. There may be elaborate and fortified gateways in the larger structures, as at the big triple-ringed fort of Garranes in county Cork. But Garranes, the excavators found, was primarily a metal workers' site, a factory producing objects like the Tara brooch, rather than a king's fortress. It is dated c AD 500.

The ring fort, called in Irish 'rath' or 'lios', or 'dun' or 'cathair (caiseal)' if built of stone, was found to be very servicable—a self-contained fortified farmstead in a country essentially rural and cityless. A 'dig' at Lough Gur in county Limerick produced a carbon 14 dating of 2,600 BC for an Early Bronze Age fort. Perhaps the majority are early Christian. Cahermacnaghten in county Clare, in the Burren, looks much like the island structures of Dun Onaght and Dun Farvagh (Inishmaan), but it was inhabited by the family of O'Davoren and their Law School down to the end of the seventeenth century.

The Christian monks adapted the secular rath to monastic use, adding chapels to the cluster of buildings inside the walls. Against unfriendly neighbours, prowling wolf-packs, or sudden brief attacks, the rath would be a good defensible place for a farmer or a monk. Cattle could, at night, be penned in the 'outer defences' of a Cahercommaun or a Dun Aengus, or in a smaller ring fort alongside. A passage in one of the legendary *Lives* of the early Irish saints suggests that many were not built by their owners but by travelling contractors. The story concerns a man whose fee for this work was sufficient cattle to fill the area between the concentric walls. Ireland then reckoned her wealth in cattle and it would be no bad pay. Professor Michael J. O'Kelly wrote in a survey of the ring-fort problem in 1970 :

> To sum up, the Irish ring fort may be an indigenous invention of the late Neolithic times. Once invented, the type continued to be built down to the seventeenth century AD, there being numerous variations in the details of construction. The ditch and bank of the *rath* and the dry-built wall of the *caiseal* or *cathair* were little more than stockyard enclosures around the house and animal shelters of a farming family. This pattern of isolated dwellings persists to the present day. Even the very

45

impressive sites are not military structures—they are merely 'big houses' of the time, their snobbish owners manifesting their wealth by building great stone walls late in the Early Christian Period.

It is interesting that an ordinary Aranman, by common observation, reached much the same conclusion as the trained archaelogist. Tom O'Flaherty, brother of the novelist Liam O'Flaherty, in a book published in 1934, remarked :

> I came to the conclusion that the builders had a keen appreciation of the value of land; for this [Eoghanacht/Onaght] and the other forts in the island command the choicest pieces of land in Aran Mor. From the tall cliffs on the south of Eoghanacht to the sloping beach on the north, there is a fairly decent pasturage, water is abundant, there are some large fields on which the soil is from four to six inches deep while the shore on the Connemara side is one of the best in the island for seaweed.

All the big stone forts of Aran have a common basic design—an immensely thick wall built of carefully fitted stones with rubble between, and, on the inside, terraces and steps so that the owners could get up to the rampart and look out. In the restoration work carried out by the Board of Works in the 1880s and 1890s it seems that some of these terraces and steps were altered, and others added. Inside, the owners had stone-built houses or huts, the beehive *clochans* of successively overlapping flags. The latter are common wherever there is plenty of suitable stone and lack of wood. They are typical of remote Celtic monastic sites and hermitages as well as of secular raths like those of Aran; the Dingle people continued to build them for outhouses almost into the present day, and in the Outer Hebrides such huts were in use as summer sheilings during the nineteenth century. Nor are they confined to Ireland and Scotland, but may be seen in other, suitably rocky, parts of Europe. In Aran they may be associated with forts and church sites, or may stand on their own.

Taking the ordinary ring forts first, there are two on Inishmore —Dun Oghil (*Dun Eochla* in Irish) and Dun Onaght (*Dun*

Eoghanacht). Dun Oghil is placed near the highest point of the island, 406ft, and the substantial ruins of the first lighthouse to be erected on the islands are close by. The fort is a massive structure, with a central enclosure surrounded by an outer ring. The inner enclosure is not quite circular, from 75 to 90ft in diameter, and the wall round it is 20ft thick. The outer enclosure comprises an area about 200ft by 250ft. Within the central enclosure neat stone piles have been made from the ruined clochans by the 'restorers'. There is a fine view over the islands and Galway Bay. The entry faces toward Kilronan and Killeany—the obvious landing places.

On the uplands round Dun Oghil are the remains of Baile na Sean, an ancient settlement of further stone ring-forts and of clochans, all of which were mapped by G. H. Kinahan in the 1860s. But as the *Shell Guide* authors say feelingly, 'the high fences obscure the monuments and make exploration difficult', and it is not very easy now to track all the ruins down. What they do indicate is that the big forts like Dun Oghil are merely the best preserved, and perhaps finest, examples of a common fortified homestead type of the islands, alongside which more of the island people lived in stone-built clochan huts.

Dun Onaght, as already noted, is placed on good land on the terraced hillside rising from the old church site at Onaght. It has a single wall, not quite round and about 90ft in diameter, and again there are clochan remains inside.

On Inisheer the long life of ring forts is strikingly demonstrated by the O'Briens locating their fine fourteenth- or fifteenth-century castle within the ancient walls of one. When seen from the air the old rath walls and the shapely castle set within them look magnificent. On the next height inland, actually the highest point, 212ft, is another castle-like tower, but this, for all that it looks almost medieval, is actually an old signal tower erected toward the end of the eighteenth century. Beside the tower are some completely indeterminate ruins, all that is left of *Cahir na mban*, the Fort of the Women.

Inishmaan, in Dun Conor, has the most magnificent ring fort

in all the islands, indeed in all Ireland. The island has a second simpler fort, D-shaped, on the hillside overlooking the present principal landing place and slipway. This is variously known as Dun Moher (*Dun an Mhothair*) or Dun Farvagh, and is about 90ft by 103ft. Its location, like so many mainland raths, is on a slope of the land among good fields, and not in any specially defensible position.

Dun Conor (*Dun Conchobhair*), however, is very much a fortress. It crowns a rise of land in almost hill-fort fashion, utilising a rocky gully on one side for its outer defences. There is a great inner citadel, containing ruined clochans, oval in outline (227ft by 115ft), whose wall rises to a height of 20ft and is some 18ft thick. From its ramparts, along which one can easily walk, there is a wide view over the other islands, and across the sea from Connemara and the Twelve Bens round to Galway and the Burren, and on to the Cliffs of Moher and the distant line of the Kerry coast and hills. Below this inner citadel is a substantial outer wall which curves round to base its two ends on the above-mentioned gully. The present field patterns follow the old lines of the defensive walls, radiating like the spokes of a wheel from the citadel. But there is no water supply, so the fort could be held against a brief raid only, and its peaceful function was to emphasise the importance of its owner, Conor. But who Conor was is unknown.

Nor have we any clue to the identity of Aengus of Dun Aengus in Inishmore. It is doubtful whether he was a Fir Bolg leader. Even our knowledge of his name hangs by the slender thread of one old man's memory. Roderick O'Flaherty knew the name for the dun and related it to the Fir Bolg story, but, when John O'Donovan came to the islands in 1839, the ordinary name for the place was Dun Mor, the Big Fort. In Killeany a very old man, Mr Wiggins, said in fact to be the oldest inhabitant, named it 'Dun Innees'; and he was the only person to use this name, the island version of Dun Aengus. So, by a curious twist of history, the name went down on the Ordnance map backed by the memory of a descendant of a Cromwellian trooper!

Nearly every visitor to Aran makes his pilgrimage to Dun Aengus, and it is certainly one of the most magnificent of Irish antiquities, indeed of Europe. The dun sits on the edge of sheer cliffs, near their highest point, and on the landward side the ground slopes up to its walls, so it is visible from many points about the island. There seems no reason to think we have here but half a fort, a cliff fall having removed the rest, for the walls seem to be designed to fit the cliff, which here forms the straight line on which a series of semicircles are based. When O'Donovan saw it in 1839, the central keep was in fairly good condition but the two outer walls were very decayed. Island boys rabbiting did much damage, but they had also unearthed (or rather un-rocked) a bronze hook thought to be a portion of a fibula. Later, a Dr March found a hinged ring of bronze with a cable decoration that he thought was fifth century AD, and also chert flakes or arrowheads. The latter inclined him to put an early date on the fort.

The 'restoration' work rebuilt the ruined walls, in T. J. Westropp's opinion without too much distortion of the original. An 18ft high wall, nearly 13ft thick, encloses the inner keep, 150ft north to south and 140ft east to west. Outside is a second, roughly semicircular, wall enclosing a space about 400ft long by 300ft across. Outside this again is a *chevaux de frise* of limestone slabs set on edge to form a kind of tank trap. There is yet another outer rampart beyond this, enclosing 11 acres and measuring some 1,300ft along the cliff edge.

Positioned as it is against unclimbable cliff and on the high ridge of Inishmore, and with large enclosures in which cattle might be corralled, Dun Aengus must have been an excellent refuge against a raid. The *chevaux de frise* would prevent a massive attack all along the rampart line, both channelling and slowing down any hostile approach. O'Flaherty said the place could hold 200 cows, O'Donovan 1,050. The *chevaux de frise* could also have made it more difficult for raiders, in the event of a break-in, driving cattle off easily, and given the owners a chance to counterattack.

John O'Donovan in the *Ordnance Survey Letters* gave an amusingly vivid account of this *chevaux de frise* :

> Some of these stones appear at a distance like soldiers making the onset, and many of them are so sharp that if one fell against them they would run him through. This army of stones would appear to have been intended . . . to answer the same purpose as the modern chevaux de frise, Turnpike or Tourniquet, now generally used in making a retrenchment to stop cavalry; but these stones were never intended to keep off horse as no horses could come near the place without 'breaking their legs'. They must have been therefore used for keeping off men, and very well adapted they are for this purpose, for a few men standing on the outer wall . . . could by casting stones kill hundreds of invaders while attempting to pass through this army of sharp stones.

The *chevaux de frise* of Dun Aengus is not unique. Doocaher, just along the cliffs, has one, as has the big circular stone fort of Ballykinvarga near Kilfenora in county Clare. Nor is the semi-circle based on a cliff edge plan unique either. It is the same as that of a stone fort on an island cliff edge—Cahercommaun in the Burren—and Cahercommaun has been fully excavated and dated c 800 AD.

Its owners were wealthy farmers, raising cattle on the Burren pastures. Just as at Dun Conor, the walls have sharp vertical joints that probably represent link-ups between different gangs of builders. The finding of a silver brooch, another zoomorphic one and an enamelled ornament were used to date Cahercommaun —but stone axes and iron implements were also found. This could mean that stone, like the Dun Aengus chert flakes, does not necessarily mean a very early date. It is quite possible that Dun Aengus is early Christian, even if not as late as Cahercommaun. I made the experiment of flying first over Cahercommaun and then over Dun Aengus to obtain an immediate comparative experience, and one can imagine that the same contractor laid them out.

Another Clare fort using a cliff edge to save building a wall right around is Caherlismacsheedy, and my own air observations of the Celtic hermitage of St Brendan on the summit of Mount Brandon at 3,127ft suggest that this has the same plan. At Mount Brandon the spring well, beehive oratory and beehive cell ruins are enclosed by a massive wall backing on to the crag line, but outside, much more faintly traced, are two encircling outer walls, also backing on to the cliffs in Dun Aengus style.

The Black Fort, Doocaher (*Dubh Cathair*), on the cliffs of Inishmore is a headland fort, another way of making use of natural features in constructing a defensive position. Long outjutting headlands are very common all along the Irish coast and a great many of them have been made into forts by putting a wall and ditch across their necks. Doocaher is a particularly fine example, with a great stone wall backed on the seaward side by nestling ruined clochans, and defended on the landward side by a *chevaux de frise* of stones. There are also some remains of buildings outside the defences and a midden of shells and bones.

The wall across the headland is some 200ft long and 20ft high. On either side the sea has undercut the cliffs into enormous caves, whose roofs reflect the opalescent glitter of the sea below. Rock falls and storm damage have, in fact, caused a good deal of destruction here. When O'Donovan arrived in 1839, there had been a particularly bad storm on the previous 7 January. He noted that there had been rows of stone houses along the headland snout beyond the present restored remains :

> One row extending along the wall and built up against it; another running from north to south for a distance of about 170ft where it originally branched into two rows, one extending south west as far as the margin of the cliff, and the other to the south east from the opposite margin, but these two rows thus branching from the main row are nearly washed away by storms and they seem to have suffered in a special manner from the late memorable storm, which hurled the waves in mountains over these high cliffs, cast rocks of amazing size over the lower ones to the east of them and sent a shower of spray across the whole island.

Today it is nearly impossible to make anything out of the ruinous stones lying on the headland snout. Inland, the rock pavements are bare, dotted with cushions of thrift (sea pink). But a letter quoted by T. G. Wilson in his book *The Irish Lighthouse Service* suggests a less barren past for the Doocaher area, as well as pointing to the ease with which a beehive stone hut can be constructed at any period of history. The letter is dated 30 May 1858, and is from James O'Flaherty to Sir William Wilde:

> Thos Derrane's sons John and Peter positively assert that their father built the Cloughan near Doon Caher—it was for storing potatoes which grew on the small patch of land immediately under it—there is no doubt of this bit of land having been growing potatoes up to the second year of the potato blithe, it is about thirty three or thirty four years back that that bit of land was just broken—The doorway was just built up with stones and then plastered with cow dung or Asses as the case might be.

There are, as already noted, a number of ruined clochans about the islands. There is a small, almost perfect, example on Inishmaan, but the finest is Clochan-na-Carraige near Kilmurvey on Inishmore.

It lies on the low ground among the fields east of the road out of Kilmurvey to Onaght, in the district known as Sruffaun. It is complete and large, rectangular within, 19ft by 7½ft, and 8ft high. It has a window as well as a door. Included in the stones used is a round granite boulder of the glacial erratic series of the islands. Whale vertebrae were found built into the wall; such bones were also found incorporated into a stone hut at Achill but whether with any significant purpose is not known. These beehive huts, when well built, are remarkably waterproof; they could, of course, be covered over with sod to give an even greater wind and water resistance.

Page 53 The coast: *(above)* Inisheer. Trawkeera Point. This picture shows the limestone pavements and the 'fields', some of which are just bare rock. SS *Plassy* was thrown by the storms well above normal tide marks, and sits there, as if to sail out to sea. Note, at her level, the storm beach of huge boulders thrown up by the big seas; *(below)* Kilronan, Inishmore, the 'capital' of the islands. Shows the recently enlarged pier, with the modern trawlers and lobster boats alongside, also the landing craft used to take heavy machinery to Inishmaan for the construction of the airfield there. Dot on foreshore between the main pier and the jetty, is the monument to the Atlantic rowers, Ridgway and Blyth. Roofless Church of Ireland church in foreground, Catholic church on right (only half in picture)

Page 54 The people: *(above)* Aran island family, three generations; *(below)* leaving church after Mass on Inishmaan

4   ARAN OF THE SAINTS

BOTH at ground level and from the air it is the great stone forts that stand out in the Aran scene. The many ancient churches—small and grey, snuggled among the rocks on the more fertile plots of land—are far less obvious. No tradition or story seem to have lingered about the great forts and their owners, but tales of the early saints are vivid and alive—not in the sense of plain factual history, of which little survives, but rather as a vivid folk memory, expressed in such phrases as 'Columcille was here', as if it was yesterday and not in the sixth century, and the retelling of the story of his arrival with continued interest in the local detail.

It does not really matter that these traditional stories are the stuff of legend rather than history. What is important is that the islanders have an unbroken folk memory reaching back to the people who first brought the message of that Catholic faith which they still hold. It is more than a memory, in fact it is an immediate reality, a person to person contact. Christianity, bringing a message of victory over death, of resurrection, new life in God, brought also the concept of the communion of saints, in which prayer can reach across the barrier of the grave, and the Aranman caught in a storm can call for help from a sixth-century saint—and get it.

It is impossible to understand the Christian attitude to the saints, and the pilgrimages to their shrines, which on the islands today are unhappily dying out, without first grasping the theological implications of a creed which affirms belief in the resurrection of the dead and the communion of saints. Superstition can, of course, creep in, but the Aran attitude to its early saints is orthodox theology. The Aranmen have forgotten all about Conor of Dun Conor but they have put Enda, Brecan and Cavan, along with John the Baptist and Mary Magdalen, in the stained glass of the windows of the church under the dun that was built in 1939.

Christianity seems to have filtered quietly into Ireland through the south-coast ports, which had good trading links with Continental Europe. There are a number of 'pre-Patrician' saints, like the still venerated Declan of Ardmore in county Waterford, and Ciaran (The Elder) of Cape Clear Island in county Cork. Small 'cells', little groups, of believers came into being. It seems quite likely that the mission of St Patrick was to weld these small groups into a nationwide movement, which was at the same time extended all over the country by Patrician preaching. Christianity probably came first to Ireland early in the fifth century, but it is not known when it came to Aran, or whether St Enda was the first to bring it.

Abroad, men had been going into the eastern deserts to live as monks, and this was a new and experimental venture in Christian experience and living. The monastic idea spread across Europe. Men like St Enda took the basic principle, of the total dedication to God of the individual monk, and then applied it to the local conditions and needs of Ireland. It was a rural land, without towns, and the self-contained monastery, on its own land, became the basic unit of the Church. Continental diocesan structures based on the city and its bishop were quite unsuitable in ancient Ireland, and the Church there became almost entirely monastic in character. Irish monks were missionaries, scholars, explorers as well as hermits, teachers and preachers. To the founders of the first Irish monasteries came many more young men, and women, anxious to live their lives close to God, and to learn all they could from the pioneers before going on to start their own monastic settlements.

The great development of Irish monasticism came in the sixth century, and the two great pioneers were Finian of Clonard in the Irish Midlands, and Enda on Inishmore in the Aran Islands. The pioneer in women's monasticism was St Brigit of Kildare.

Enda was, it appears, a 'late vocation', what ancient Ireland called an 'ex-layman'. He was the son of Ainmire, son of Ronan of the Cremthanns (Meath), who trained as a soldier and succeeded to his father's little kingdom. His sister Faenche, however, became a nun, influencing her brother, and on her advice, after making a foundation of his own at Ardee in county Louth, he went to learn more about the monastic way of life in Scotland, at St Ninian's famous and early foundation of Whithorn— 'Candida Casa' in Galloway. He then returned to Ireland via the port of Drogheda and, after making some foundations in the Boyne valley, took the road west, again, so it is said, urged on by his sister. He is alleged to have been given a grant of the Aran Islands by the King of Cashel, Angus mac Nadfraich, a suspect story; certainly he arrived there and settled on the good sandy land behind the strands at what was ever after to be named Enda's Church, Killeany.

Killeany was in the Irish phrase to be 'the place of his resurrection', his final great foundation, where he died, perhaps about 520, and where he is buried. Enda's own reputation and that of his rapidly growing monastery became known all over Ireland, and tradition makes most of the great saints and monastic founders of early Ireland come to Aran to visit Enda and study at his monastery. There was Columcille (Columba), who would ultimately go to Scotland and settle on the island of Iona; there was Brendan of Clonfert, en route for an adventurous exploratory voyage; and there was Ciaran (the Younger), whose foundation of Clonmacnois on the River Shannon would perhaps become the most famous of all early Irish monasteries. The legends of the Irish saints have scant respect for chronology, and Enda must have been long dead when some of those supposed to have met him came to Aran. But it is very probable that a large number did come at various dates to the famous pioneering monastery at Killeany, and then go on to make their own foundations elsewhere.

The kind of monastic life these men were living was much closer to that of the early 'Desert Fathers' than to modern western religious life, which is organised, minutely legislated and diversi-

fied. It was very similar, however, to modern Orthodox monasticism, which has remained close to monastic origins, and is still
an undifferentiated straightforward monastic dedication and
living, one in which the hermit life is seen as the final goal. Just so
in early Ireland, for you can still find ancient ruined hermitages
on islands and hillsides; though even then, as with some near
contemporary Orthodox holy men, the hermit was forced to return
from the wilds to the crowds, who came to seek his help and
advice. Prayer, fasting, vigil, and work form the staple of this
way of life, as they did in Enda's time on Aran.

Similarly, prayer, fasting and vigil, have remained the staple in-
gredients of traditional Irish pilgrimages right into our own day.
Aran people still spend the night of St Cavan's feast day at the
site of his monastery and church on Inisheer.

All over the Aran Islands are the remains of these early churches
and monastic sites, but the actual ruins do not go back to St Enda's
time, though some are very early. They span a long period of
Irish church history from virtually the first Christian centuries to
the Reformation. The early Celtic Church liked to build several
small churches rather than one huge edifice, so at the ancient sites
there are normally groups of churches. As time went on, they
were enlarged and/or rebuilt, so that the architecture, even on
very ancient sites, may be of many different periods. Crosses were
also set up in the monastic enclosure, or to mark its lands outside.
To begin with, the cross was cut on any suitable unshaped boulder,
but as time went on the cross and the designs that decorated the
surrounding rock took more and more command; the stone was
shaped to a pillar and then into a cross; and in the tenth century
there was the final flowering in the great sculptured 'high crosses',
with their carefully worked out sequences of pictures showing
God's help to man, and liturgical sequences for the great festivals
of the year.

With St Malachy came the introduction of the Cistercians, a
Continental religious order, and the Canons Regular of St Augus-
tine, who were 'secular' clergy living in community rather than
monks in the full sense of the word. The 1170 Anglo-Norman

invasion helped the introduction of more Continental religious orders into Ireland and halted the reform and renewal that seems to have been going on in the native monastic and church tradition. The Canons Regular took over many of the old Celtic monastic establishments, and it is said they came to Aran. Later the Franciscans had a house at Killeany.

Both the Franciscan friary and most of St Enda's group of churches went into the rebuilding of the nearby Arkyn Castle by the Cromwellian forces and others who garrisoned it. In fact, the fragments of the high cross now in St Enda's church were reclaimed from Killeany Castle and house walls.

The site of the great pioneering monastery of St Enda of Aran is on the strand edge between the airfield at Killeany and the eastern tip of Inishmore. Sea and sand have encroached on it, and it is marked by the great mound of a burial ground at the tide's edge. However, as the stump of the round tower and the shaft of a high cross are in the fields just behind Killeany, and little Temple Benan is up on the ridge above, the monastic 'city', to use the Irish phrase, must have sprawled over a great deal of land. Tradition says 120 holy people are buried in the graveyard. In 1645 the Archbishop of Tuam, Malachy O'Cadhla (latinised Malachias Qualeus), made a list of the diocese's churches, including those at Killeany. They were Killenda (St Enda's Church), Teglach Enda (St Enda's House), Teampall mac longa, Teampall mic Canoinn, St Mary's and Temple Benan. Teampall, from the Latin, is one of several Irish words for a church. All except Teglach Enda and St Benan's, whose stones were too far away to be worth dragging down, went into the castle building at Arkyn.

Teglach Enda still stands in the old graveyard where St Enda is buried. It is a small well preserved but roofless early church, which has outjutting buttresses called *antae*, characteristic of many early Irish churches and possibly derived from the heavy woodwork of timber buildings. Inside, some of the surviving inscribed stones from the old graveyard have been mortared to the altar for preservation, and the fragments of the high cross are set upright, cemented togther one above the other. Slabs with crosses and sometimes a request for a prayer were, in ancient Ireland, laid on people's graves. Here one inscription is given in very abbreviated form—BEN (dach) T DIE F(or) AN(main) S(an)C(t)AN (Blessing of God on the soul of Sanctan). Another reads OROIT AR SCANDLAN (Pray for Scandlan). Near the stump of the round tower stands the high cross shaft, elaborately carved with interlacing animals, frets and knots; the portions in Teglach Enda include a fine carving of a man on a horse. Probably such a large monastic site would have had several elaborately carved crosses. There is the equally richly carved shaft of another cross at the 'Seven Churches' site at Onaght at the other end of Inishmore.

A study by Liam de Paor in the early 1950s of these limestone high crosses of Aran and of the adjacent county Clare led to the conclusion that there was a definite local school of sculptors. The fret seen on the Clare and Aran crosses seems peculiar to this local workshop. Liam de Paor thought the style had perhaps originated in Aran, the sculptors later moving to Clare. He traced both Scottish and Viking influences and thought the sculptor could have come from, or had some connection with, Scotland, and, curiously, with eastern Scotland. 'The carvings of the horsemen at Killeany and Kilfenora (Co. Clare) much more closely resemble the carvings of horsemen on the slabs at Hilton of Cadboll or Rossie Priory than they do those on the crosses of Kells or Clonmacnois. A connection of some sort between the eastern Scottish monuments and the Clare and Aran crosses is indicated, although the resemblances should not be overstressed.' De Paor dated the crosses to the second half of the eleventh century.

St Benan's church, Temple Benan, or, as it is sometimes called, Teampall Mionnain, is probably the most exciting and oldest church building on the islands. Its two steep cats-eared gables stand out on the rocky skyline behind Killeany, and it is complete except for the roof. It is built in massive stonework in very early style, and is small and solid. It has a narrow door with inclined jambs and a massive lintel stone across them, and the tiny east window's head and splay are cut from a single rock. The dimensions of this perfectly proportioned little chapel are 15ft 1in by 11ft 3in externally, 10ft 9in by 7ft internally, and the gables are 15ft high. The lintel stone over the door is 6ft long, and the door is 5ft 6in high, narrowing from 1ft 9in wide at the step to 1ft 3in at the lintel. Benan himself was an early disciple of St Patrick and succeeded him at Armagh, where he died in 467. He is regarded as the patron of Connacht, and, as he is said to have evangelised both in Clare and Kerry, he could have had some personal connection with Aran, perhaps with the first preaching of Christianity there.

Beside the chapel on the hillside are some now very ruinous clochans and a cashel, supposedly of monastic origin. A stone inscribed CARI is built into the wall of St Benan's and a cross-inscribed gravestone found nearby reads OR (oit) AR MAINACH (Pray for Manach).

The stone forts might be waterless, but the early monastic sites were always close to springs and streams, and the former would come in due course to be venerated as holy wells. The Killeany district has several—Dabhach Einne (St Enda's well); and Tobar na mBrathar, the friars' well.

The stump only remains of the round tower, well built of carefully hewn stone. O'Donovan says that it once stood five stories high, according to tradition. These round towers were part bell tower (the small handbells of the early Irish church had a long carry when rung from that height), part refuge, and probably also part look-out. By shutting the single door, which was often well up the tower side and reached by a ladder that could be pulled in after one, the monks had an excellent refuge during a brief raid. The tradition that O'Donovan recorded implies that the islanders knew the tower had been a belfry. They said the bell was buried near St Enda's well.

There are a few scattered references to Aran and Killeany in the Irish Annals—a disastrous fire in 1020, an attack by the Vikings in 1081, and the death of the last abbot, Donatus O'Leyn, in 1400. The Franciscan foundation is said to have been made in 1485, but no history of it seems to have been recorded.

The second large monastic site of Inishmore is the 'Seven Churches' of Onaght, at the western end of the island. It was a sheltered site in a valley with a stream running through it, and wild garlic now grows thickly over the old graveyard and ruins. Few, if any, early Irish sites have seven churches, and the name was given later in romantic fantasy around the mystical number seven. The Onaght site is actually a complex of two churches and domestic buildings of various dates, and has a fine cross shaft, now on the tomb of its founder saint, Brecan, and an important series of early inscribed cross pillars.

Little is known about St Brecan. One account makes him the son of Eochy Ballderg, King of Thomond. He is said to have been a monk of St Enda's community and to have succeeded Enda as abbot there. If he did, it is surprising that he did not remain at Killeany and be buried there. Whatever the details of his history, Brecan arrived at Onaght, founded his monastery in this well watered, fertile and sheltered site, and left a reputation for sanctity that has remained evermore in popular memory.

The first of the two churches on the site, St Brecan's Church, Teampall Bhreacain, is a large building close to the saint's grave. It seems to have originated in the eighth century, with *antae*, to which a chancel was added in the tenth century, when the older building was enlarged. You can still see the lines of the original gable end in the present western gable. The south door is late medieval. Built into the wall inside the church is a slab incribed OR AR II CANOIN (Pray for two canons). The second church of the complex is upstream, where the little valley narrows, and is the fifteenth-century Teampall an Phoill, a name perhaps meaning the Church of the Hollow. It is probably of the same period as the latest of the domestic buildings.

The cross-inscribed pillar stones have now been collected into a group, and the readings found on them are printed on notices beside them. These stones are, of course, of very much earlier date than the fragment of an elaborate high cross on Brecan's grave. The most interesting inscriptions read TOMAS AP, taken to refer to Thomas the Apostle, and VII ROMANI (Seven Romans). The latter could refer to the cult of the seven martyred sons of Symphorosa, a family of early martyrs known and venerated in ancient Ireland; or to some of the many 'overseas students' and pilgrims who came to Ireland's famous schools and monasteries, some of whom settled and finally died there. Outside the group of buildings is a 'station', a cairn of stones, called *Leaba an Spioraid Naoimh* (the Bed or Station of the Holy Spirit), and an early cross slab inscribed s(an) c(t) I BRE(ca)NI(Saint Brecan). Another stone asks a prayer for the soul of Scandlan—ORAIT AR ANMAIN SCANDLAIN.

Here at Onaght, with Dun Onaght on the hillside above, and the ruins of a square, much later, castle across a couple of fields (Sean Caislean, Old Castle), there was obviously a large and important monastery in early times. Its useful life must have extended over a long period to judge by the date of the latest of the surviving ruins. It may not, for the final centuries, have been a full monastic institution but a church served by several clergy.

Devotion to St Brecan lived on, and until very recently there was a pilgrimage or 'pattern' (from the word patron, for patron saint) here, with an overnight vigil. Traditional Irish pilgrimages follow a common rule of making 'rounds' to a series of 'stations'—a church, a well, a saint's grave, or a cross—walking right-handed sunwise a set number of circles and saying a set number of prayers. The right-handed round may be linked with ancient sun-worship, and, as with Christian worship elsewhere, veneration for the sun has been diverted to that of the Sun of Justice, the unsetting Light, Jesus Christ. The left-handed round is unlucky, the circuit one makes to curse rather than to bless. The traditional prayers are the short prayers everyone knows by heart—the Lord's Prayer, Hail Mary, Glory be to the Father, the Creed. These are said over and over again at each 'station', perhaps, on the longer pilgrimages like the still very flourishing one at Lough Derg on the mainland, many hundreds of times. Traditionally one keeps count with pebbles or other easily gathered counters; more recently rosary beads have been used, and sometimes the recitation of the rosary is substituted for the traditional sets of prayers. An overnight vigil may be held—it still is at Lough Derg, and it used to be at Onaght. At the latter the women kept vigil on St Brecan's 'bed' within the group of buildings, while the men spent the night in the field outside. In 1971 an elderly man in the district recalled keeping this overnight vigil in his youth, but the custom has now died out. In fact the only really active Inishmore pilgrimage, and that no longer draws crowds, seems to be to St Columcille's well at Killeany on 9 June.

In earlier times the islanders made a round of the entire island of Inishmore, visiting all its holy places, on Holy Thursday and Good Friday. This ceremony was still going on when O'Donovan visited the island in 1839, and he was told that some fourteen years previously, with the priest's consent, Brecan's grave at Onaght was opened by a visiting Spaniard, Don Pedro, and a stone marked with an inscription, the Head of Brecan, carried away by an antiquary.

Between the great monastic sites at Onaght and Killeany stretch a whole series of early churches along the fertile side of Inishmore. Beside Kilmurvey, in a field from which one looks up to Dun Aengus, is an ancient ruined chapel called Teampall na Naomh, church of the saint, but nothing is known of its history. At Kilmurvey stands the church of St Colman MacDuagh. That saint flourished in the seventh century, his principal foundation being at Kilmacdaugh near Gort, where a fine group of old churches and a round tower still remain. He also made a foundation up in the Burren hills, at Oughtmama, and another on Aran. There is a tall cross-inscribed pillar stone outside the west door of the church. The west end has a door with a massive stone lintel and the walls on either side project in *antae*. This 'nave' is the original church, of the eighth or ninth centuries, to which a later Romanesque chancel was added, the two being linked by a fine circular arch. The most curious feature appears on the north wall near the west end, where a horse has been sculpted on the corner of a massive block of stone forming part of the

64

church's masonry. There are some traces of a surrounding cashel wall, for monastic etablishments, as already noted, had a wall round them like the secular forts. O'Donovan was told of the tradition that there was a wall round all the Onaght churches, which is very likely true.

On the hill, a little above the present main road from Kilmurvey to Kilronan, in the Cowrugh area, is the little fifteenth-century church of the Four Beautiful Saints, Teampall an Cheathrair Aluinn. The 'Four Beauties' are Brendan of Birr, Fursey, Conall and Berchan, but why this church should be dedicated to them, and why they should have been called beautiful, is not known. Brendan of Birr was a contemporary of Brendan of Clonfert, the 'Voyager'. Fursey was one of the great Continental missionary saints, and is mentioned by the Venerable Bede in his *History*. Fursey went first to England and later to the Continent, and while in England he fell ill and had a vision of heaven and hell; his account of the experience seems to have triggered off the series of such visions of which Dante's is the most famous. Berchan is called by the ancient *Martyrology of Oengus* 'Fer da lethe' (man of two sides), because like many Irish saints he spent part of his time in Ireland and part in Scotland—where he was later to be remembered and venerated in various places.

Behind the ruined church is the well of the Four Beauties, Bollan an Cheathrair Aluinn—the 'Well of the Saints' of Synge's play. Its water was supposed to be good for eye diseases and epilepsy. Some people evidently still visit it—within a few months of Ireland going decimal, the 'Well of the Saints' had done so, too, and the new coinage was being tossed into its clear water.

On the very fertile land, beside good springs and below the level of the main road, along the minor road running close to the south-east shore are two more old churches. One is Teampall Assurnaidhe, the Church of St Soorney, a female saint according to local tradition. There is a projecting 'handle stone' at one corner of the little church; such stones are found at a few other early Irish churches. St Soorney's well is not far off. But Monaster Kieran (Mainister Chiarain), St Ciaran's (of Clonmacnois)

Monastery, or Monaster Chonannachtach (the Connacht Monastery), is the more important of the two sites in this area. Again there is an early church, perhaps of eighth- or ninth-century date, with a primitive west door; the east window, whose mouldings end in grotesque heads, is a twelfth-century Romanesque addition, and the north doorway may be late medieval.

On the outside of Monaster Kieran are two interesting cross-inscribed pillar stones. Outside the west door is a tall and slender pillar with a simple yet sophisticated cross design cut on it. Beyond the east end is a stumpier pillar, whose design includes a circle and a hole through the top of the stone; rags used to be passed through the hole and then used as 'cures', but its original purpose was almost certainly to hold the gnomen of a sundial. Stone pillars with sundials are known from other Irish Celtic Church monastic sites, like Kilmalkedar in county Kerry. The latter is marked in three-hour periods, the times of the canonical hours of prayer; the Monaster Kieran stone has simply a circular undivided dial, but it has been suggested that the time scale was painted on to this. It would then have recorded Prime (6 o'clock), Terce (9 o'clock), None (12 o'clock), Sext (15 o'clock) and Vespers (18 o'clock), the times at which the 'Hours' of the Divine Office should be recited.

Some way from the church is an old graveyard and a couple of tall cross pillars, with plain Latin crosses cut on them and slight bulges at the cross arms; they suggest termon crosses marking the boundary of the monastery enclosure. There are also a couple of tall *gallauns* near the Church of the Four Beauties, said by some traditions to mark the graves of holy men but possibly ancient Megalithic standing stones. They have no symbols cut on them.

A peculiar feature of contemporary Aran devotion to the early saints is that, although Enda was one of the most important of the early Church leaders and his monastery of key importance in the development of Irish monasticism, it is Columcille (Columba) who is foremost in people's minds, and it is to his well at Killeany they still make pilgrimage. Yet Columcille was, at most, only a brief visitor to Aran. Manus O'Donnell, who collected all he could find, historical and legendary, about Columcille in his

Betha Colaim Chille (Life of Columcille) of 1532, tells a little tale about the saint on Aran which, though pure fancy and belonging to a *genre* of legend told of many saints, has in a strange way come true.

'On a time' writes Manus, 'Columcille went to visit Ara of the Saints where dwelt Enne of Ara and many other holy men.' Columcille asked Enda for a portion of the island, but Enda refused because he thought that Columcille was so great a saint that the whole island would come to be called after him. But Columcille persisted : 'So lief and dear to me is this island that I would bless it. And that some portion thereof might be called after me, I would fain get from you a portion, small or great thereof'. Enda still refused, until Columcille asked merely for the width of his hood. But the hood began to spread and spread and Enda snatched it up before it covered all Aran. Columcille was angry and spoke a word picture of an island paradise, which, owing to Enda's interference, Aran would never be. He said :

The isle shall be the worse therefor, for if thou hadst suffered me to bless it, there had come thereto no ship save a ship that came with pilgrims, and there had been no port where a ship might come to, save one port only, in that place that is called Acaill. And one man might have defended it against ships of the men of the world. And no stranger nor foreigner had come there ever. And he that had done shame or evil there, his two soles should have stuck to the soil of the island, so that he might not have taken one step until he made good that shame. And it had been a burying ground for the hosts of the Western World. And there had been a throng of birds of paradise sing-ing there each day. And there had been no sickness nor dis-temper upon the folk there save the sickness of death. And the taste of its water had been mixed with honey, and its fields and harvests without sowing or plowing and labor from them save the labor of harvest. And the folk of this island had had no need of kine save one cow for each house. And they had had from her their fill of milk and the fill of their guests. And the bells had struck of themselves at the hour of the masses and of the hours, and the candles been enlumined of themselves at the mass and in the midst of the night when the saints were saying their

hours. And there had been no lack of turf for laying a fire again
forever in that place. And since I have not left my blessing,
belike there shall be every want thereon whereof we have made
mention.

'And all that came to pass as Columcille had said', adds Manus
O'Donnell. 'And in especial it came to pass touching the laying
of the fires, for the folk on that island have nor turf nor fire-wood
from that time till this, but they do make fire of cow-dung only,
dried in the sun.'

Curse or blessing, Columcille remains the great saint of
Inishmore.

There are a couple of early church sites on Inishmaan, across
Gregory's Sound. A ruined tower in drystone, called Turmartin,
on the Inishmore cliff side in this area is said to mark the grave
of St Gregory, who is supposed to have been a local saint. In the
centre of Inishmaan, in the fertile hollow under Dun Conor, is
the ancient church site of Teampall na Seacht mic Righ, the
Church of the Seven Sons of the King. This is close to the present
Catholic church, and to the site, just across the road, of St Mary's
church, Teampall Muire, which was a fifteenth-century building
with a modern transept that the islanders used for Mass until
their new church was opened in 1939. The Seacht mic Righ site
has the foundations of an early building, which was 'nearly gone'
when Westropp saw it, though he was able to take its measure-
ments of 41ft by 22ft. Beside the site is the cairn of stones and
stone cross marking the burying place of St Kennerg, said to have
been the daughter of a King of Leinster. The islanders used to
hold this Aharla na Kennirge (grave of Kennerg) in great veneration, but no longer go to pray there.

One suspects that the whole complex of St Mary's church, the
Church of the Seven Princes and St Kennerg's tomb belong to a
single old monastic site that sprawled over both sides of the
modern road. It was well placed to form a comfortable and
sheltered settlement.

All but the roof remains of the tiny but solid Cill Chean-
nannach, Kilcananagh or Temple Kenanagh, at the landing slip

at Cora Point. The church, circled by a graveyard paved with nineteenth-century slab tombstones, sits on a level plat behind which the next step of the terraced island flank rises up in great rounded shoulders of grey limestone. Each terrace here has good land on it. Erected before AD 1000, the church is built of big blocks, with walls 2ft thick, though it measures a mere 16ft by 9ft 6in. Outside are projecting corbels or 'handles' which, it is suggested, may have supported roof timbers, end rafters or barge boards. There are various traditions and theories about the name of this little church, which may just mean Church of the Canons. One island tradition says the name is that of the mother of the seven saints or princes of the other church site on the island, but another identifies Kenanagh with Gregory of the Sound.

Across on Inisheer, Teampall na Seacht mic Righ is, perhaps deliberately matched with Cill na Seacht n-Inion (or Inghean), the Church of the Seven Daughters. When O'Donovan saw it, the place was very ruinous, but the Board of Works rebuilt it with some energy in 1889. It is still hard to find among island stone walls and hard to see from ground level. There is a massive semi-circle of heavy cashel-style wall at the back, upslope, and below it ruins of cells or beds and a cross-inscribed pillar stone supposed to mark the grave of the Seven Daughters.

From the air the site makes much more sense. The curving horseshoe of monastic enclosure wall shows up clearly against the rectangular pattern of the ordinary island fields, with the old cell and grave ruins at the 'mouth' of the horseshoe curve. Cill na Seacht n-Inion becomes interesting, instead of one of the least important, of the Aran island sites when seen from the air, for the monastic cashel wall, paralleling the cashel wall of the secular fortified homestead, the stone fort, can be readily seen encircling most of an ancient site.

Tobar Einne, St Enda's well, at the north end of Inisheer is still visited by island people on Sundays. Also at the north end is St Gobnet's church, with a ruined clochan beside it. Outside this early little oratory, which is well preserved, is a *bullaun* stone of ice-carried granite that probably served as a form of primitive mortar. Gobnet is one of Ireland's best loved women saints, and there is massive devotion to her at the 'place of her resurrection', Ballyvourney in county Cork, though little is known about her. She may have lived sometime in the sixth century, and it is said that she fled from her home in county Clare to Inisheer to escape some enemy. On the island an angel appeared and told her that the 'place of her resurrection' would be where she found nine white deer grazing. So she left Aran and travelled across southern Ireland, finding increasing numbers of white deer and leaving a string of church foundations, until she came to Ballyvourney, where there were nine white deer among the trees on the hillside, so she settled down permanently, to organise her little convent there. She is said to have been a skilled beekeeper, and to have successfully outwitted a robber who had taken her little herd of cattle by loosing her bees on him.

St Gobnet's church is set on a level flat of grass in a sun-warmed hollow of Inisheer's flank. The other churches are down on the sand, one entirely lost. The list of island churches made by the archbishop in 1645 says Inisheer had a church of St Paul, and Westropp was told by the islanders of a 'Killanybeg' lost in the sands—probably the same church. St Cavan's church has not shared a like fate simply because of energetic and constant digging. In 1971 the dunes rose round it as high as the gables and the ancient little church was cradled in a bed of soft sand. In O'Donovan's time the islanders went each Sunday to pray there, and today they still hold a big annual pilgrimage on the saint's day, 14 June, when the Mass is celebrated at the old church.

Teampall Chaomhain has been compared to the Trinity Church at Glendalough in county Wicklow. St Caomhen or Cavan was the brother of St Kevin of Glendalough, it is claimed, but few, if any, certainties are known about his life. The present chancel of the little church in the sand dunes is tenth century, with a nave added perhaps a century or so later. The doorway of the old church, with its heavy stone lintel, was re-inserted in the new west wall. The head of the chancel arch, the pointed arch of the doorway in the south wall, and the sacristy are late medieval.

Page 71 Some islanders: *(above) Dun Aengus* on a fair day at Inisheer with bullock prepared for embarkation; *(left and right)* two typical Aranmen

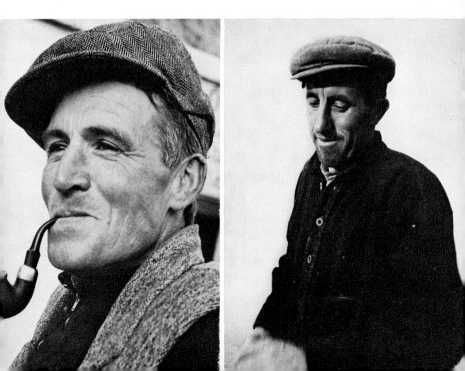

Page 72 Roads: *(above)* 'the Seven Churches' of Onaght, Inishmore. Just above the road running across the middle of the picture are the ruins of St Brecan's Church, and, higher up, in the neck of the little valley, the second, later church, of the group. The other buildings were domestic ones of the monastic settlement. St Brecan's grave or 'bed' is the square right of the gable end of the large church. The curving field wall, left of the church group, might follow the curving line of the original monastic enclosure wall. An old castle ruin lies to the bottom left corner of the photo; *(below)* the main road of Inishmaan

St Caomhen's grave lies north-east of the church and is covered by blown sand (1971), and sand runs right up to the old graveyard and the church.

Just as with Gobnet, even if little is known of his personal history, Cavan was a real man, to whom Inisheer people have turned for help for centuries. At Ballyvourney it is claimed that Gobnet's intercession brings answers to prayer, and cures; so too with Cavan on Inisheer. It is, of course, notoriously difficult to 'prove' a miraculous cure, but as far as the patient is concerned the matter is simple enough : 'I was sick, now I am well'.

Roderick O'Flaherty (1684) says that Inisheer was also called Ara Choemain, Cavan's Island. The distribution of sand and grass was rather different then. At the old church, he says, 'there is a marble stone over his [Cavan's] tomb with a square wall built about it on a plain green field in prospect of the sea, where sick people used to lie overnight and recover health of God for his [Cavan's] sake. I have seen one grievously tormented by a thorn thrust into his eye, who, by so lying in Saint Coemhan's burying place, had it miraculously taken out without the least feeling of the patient, a mark whereof remains to this day in the corner of his eye'.

St Cavan was also much called upon for help in storm and fog at sea. Nurse Hedderman, the first nurse on the island, whose book of experiences was published in 1917, had to struggle against island superstitions, folk 'cures' and poverty. But she went to the trouble of collecting stories of some of the alleged cures brought about by St Cavan's intercession. The mother of a child with what appeared to have been acute meningitis, whom the doctor had given up, went to the saint's grave and would not leave it. She had the half-conscious child carried on the 'rounds' of the church, and it suddenly recovered and ran home cured. And hospital-trained Nurse Hedderman, in the final desperation of a case when no doctor could be found, and a half starved old woman in a cold house seemed to be dying with acute inflammatory rheumatism and complications that pointed to pericarditis, tried prayer. The woman's family promised prayers to St Cavan

E

and some of her relatives went to the church. That evening the patient was a little better, in three weeks time well again. Tough island constitutions, or the power of prayer? The answer is anybody's guess, but the woman was well again.

John O'Donovan, in the *Ordnance Survey Letters* of 1839, adds a final, rather touching detail of island Christianity, as it then was. 'The islanders', he records, 'also carry a paper containing the first verses of the gospel of St John, in token of their belief in the Divinity of Christ.'

5   THE GARRISON ISLAND

ARAN history is a tantalising series of flashes of information
with no continuous light on day to day affairs until the
nineteenth century. The ruins of the churches indicate
a long and important ecclesiastical history—most of them remained in use and repair until the Reformation. The islands'
secular history was important, too, but is even more difficult to
study in any detail.

The islands seem to have been more orientated towards county
Clare than county Galway in the Middle Ages and they were part
of the lordship of the Clare family of O'Brien. On Inisheer, the
O'Briens' (or Furmina) Castle still stands inside the walls of the
old dun. They had another, more important, castle at Arkyn
at Killeany, but this was to be entirely rebuilt and enlarged by
subsequent island garrisons. Nothing now remains of Arkyn
Castle but the long wall fronting the sea at Killeany pier.

The Inisheer castle is a good example of a late medieval Irish
tower house or small castle, a type very common all over the
country and very much like Scottish border peel towers. They
are a product of the civilisation that developed after the coming
and assimilation of the Normans, and like the ring forts, such
as the very 'dun' in which Furmina stands, are fortified houses
rather than castles capable of withstanding long sieges. On the
Scottish borders and all over Ireland one needed a strong house
that could be easily defended against raids, when the marauders
were more anxious to carry off cattle than capture it.

Furmina shows the typical plan of such tower houses—massive
walls, the vaulted ground floor, and the ruins of the rooms above,
which were the full breadth and width of the tower and were

75

reached by stone stairs in the thickness of its wall. Wooden floors alternated with one or more stone floors over the vaulted ground floor. Sometimes there is a little decoration on the outer wall—Furmina has a human face carved on a projecting stone. It is still possible to scramble on to its battlements and gain a wide view over the islands, the sea and the mainland.

There is also the square ruin of Sean Caislean at Onaght, which might be sixteenth century in date. We do not know when people on the islands ceased living in the great stone forts, though at least one in county Clare was occupied to the end of the seventeenth century.

Irish history is notoriously complex, yet some attempt must be made to give an outline into which the series of references to Aran can be fitted. It was the Vikings, when they settled, who introduced towns to rural Ireland, and in 1170 came the Anglo-Norman invasion of men also accustomed to town life. But it was then, even as it still is, possible for the stranger to become 'more Irish than the Irish themselves' and the old Gaelic culture reasserted itself over most of the country, though mingled with some of the incomers' influences and customs.

Galway became a walled city from 1270, an enclave of people of a different culture and language from the Gaelic world around them. It was an important town, trading with France and Spain, and it had an agreement with the O'Briens, who were, it is thought, the lords of the Aran Islands for some 450 years, to protect this valuable trade. For Aran is the key to the shipping routes in the area, as already noted, and the city of Galway was glad to pay the O'Briens 12 tuns of wine annually for coastguard patrol. There are records of agreements for this wine payment in 1280 and 1308. In 1334 the Lord Justice, the English Sir John Darcy, with the considerable force of fifty-six ships, pillaged the Aran Islands. Again, in 1388, the islands appear in another brief record when they joined with Galway in a rising against the Crown, and a burgess of Galway, Nicholas Kent, went to England to commission ships from the Bristol merchants to fight them. In 1400 he had a licence to attack Galway and the Aran Islands with four ships; the licence stated that the Aran Islands were full of galleys waiting to capture English ships. But later the leader of the rising, Clanrickarde, made peace, and Kent's licence was withdrawn.

With the coming of the Tudors and the Reformation, there was a reconquest of Ireland. It was massively mounted and successful; among the leaders of those who became grantees or grabbers of Irish land were Sir Walter Raleigh and Edmund Spenser. 'Planting' of Ireland with incomers began. This fighting had a new bitterness, for it was no longer English against Irish but Protestant against Catholic, and men began to die for their faith as well as their country. The O'Briens now lost the Aran Islands to the O'Flahertys from Connemara. On 25 May 1582 Elizabeth I granted Murrogh Na doe O'Flaherty the fee farm on the islands, despite the mayor and corporation of Galway petitioning her in support of their old allies, the O'Briens.

In the middle of this turmoil, Grainne Ui Maille (Grace O'Malley), the bold and independent ruler of Clare Island to the north, came raiding. The *State Papers* record (April 1590) how she, 'with two or three baggage boats full of thieves, not knowing peace was declared, committed some spoil on the Isle of Aran to the value of 20 marks, which she did by persuasion of some of the O'Flahertys soon after Sir Thomas L'Estrange was dead'. For Elizabeth did not leave the islands long in O'Flaherty hands; according to her, they belonged to the Crown, and she could dispose of them as she liked. She granted them by letters patent dated 13 January 1587 to John Rawson of Athlone and his heirs, on condition they retained a posse of twenty English soldiers on the islands. Later the ownership passed to Sir Roebuck Lynch of Galway.

Inquisitions were made into the ownership and divisions of land and property in 1594 and 1616. They seem to have been taken in Arkyn Castle, and the inquisition of 1594 gives an interesting list of placenames of the 'Iles of Aran' or 'Insulae Sanctorum' (Islands of Saints). The three islands are named as Arenmore, Inishmaine and Inish Eraght. A source for Aran personal names are the Fiants (warrants) of Elizabeth I for the period 1590 to 1600, when many islanders, mostly labourers, are listed as being pardoned for rebellion.

The Aran Islands reached their height of strategic importance during the wars of the mid-seventeenth century. At first Ireland was fighting for the Catholic cause against king and parliament, and then against Cromwell. The Confederation of Kilkenny of 1642 fought for the restoration of the Catholic Faith to Ireland, and some kind of agreement with the English King to that effect. Charles I had his own troubles at home, and in 1649 Cromwell arrived in Dublin and began the savage Irish war of extermination and plantation by his followers that is still a live memory. It is said that about five-sixths of the population of Ireland either died or fled the country during the ten years of war in Confederate and Cromwellian times.

Galway was extremely important as an entry port at this time, and the Aran Islands were accordingly fortified and garrisoned first by one side and then by the other. In a description of Connacht by Oliver St John in 1614, in the Carew MSS, there is a contemporary estimate of their value :

> The road in the Isles of Aran called Gregory's Sound wherein a hundred ships of good burthen may ride at any time. An enemy possessing this sound may be master of all the isles of Aran (which are well inhabited) and command all the bay (of Galway). It may be saved by building a fort in the Great Island and be of great use and importance. It was therefore projected and the late Queen gave a liberal allowance of land etc. for the building of it, but according to the usual fate of this kingdom, it was not looked after, and so cast away. The English, Britons (Bretons) and Portugalles (in times past) had a great trade of fishing here for cod, ling, hake and conger, which would continue still if it were undertaken.

In the *Clanrickarde Memoirs* a letter from Clanrickarde (who became a supporter of the royal Stuarts), dated 11 February 1641, to the Earl of Thomond again notes the importance of the islands. 'Amongst all, I find none more necessary to be preserved than the isles of Arran. These are in the possession of Sir Roebuck

Lynch, son to Sir Henry. I am now informed that Boetius Clancy the younger and the Clan Teige of Thomond under pretence of some antiquated claims, intend to invade it, and request that you take steps to prevent it.' In May 1642 Clanrickarde informed the Lord Justices that Sir Roebuck had had his isles surprised and taken from him, and in October of the same year the Mayor of Galway gave details—the islands had been plundered by one Captain Willoughby and his ships, and Sir Roebuck had, accordingly, lost his £400 annual rent.

In the war with Cromwell Clanrickarde hoped to hold the islands as a base to accommodate troops and supplies promised by the Duke of Lorraine. This help never came, and the islands were taken, but in 1651 he sent 200 men, with officers and a gunner, to hold the islands. They failed, surrendering in January 1652. The Cromwellians made the O'Briens' castle on Inisheer unusable, and rebuilt Arkyn, using the stones ready to hand in the Killeany churches and Franciscan friary. In fact the doorway in the still-standing section of east wall at the old castle was probably taken direct from the friary.

The Cromwellians did not establish themselves on the islands without some Irish attempt to retake them. The Commissioners to the Committee of Irish Affairs reported on 20 December 1652 :

> Reports on the descent upon a garrison of yours, in Aran, by 600 men from Boffin, who with the assistance of the inhabitants, seized it. They were helped by the weakness of the works which were not yet finished but mainly by want of ships in the harbour to assist. The ships appointed here, contrary to orders, put out to sea. Because of the importance of Aran and because of its future strength whenever the enemy shall have finished the fortifications already begun, 1500 men are ordered there and three to four ships from Kinsale via Galway, with provisions as none are to be had in Galway.

On 9 January 1653, 1,300 foot soldiers and a battery piece were shipped to Aran, under the command of Major-General Reynolds, on board the *Sun*, and 600 men sent to west Connacht from Galway as a reinforcement if it was needed. Aran surrendered on 15 January.

The fortifications were completed and the island used as a concentration camp for some forty to fifty Catholic priests, who were allowed 6d a day to live on. The Ormond Papers at 19 March 1660 note the sum of £44 17s 6d due to Major John Allen for monies distributed by him to the priests on Aran. A letter to Ormond dated 1680 says that at the time of the Restoration there were only forty priests in Ireland, all of whom were on Aran. This is hardly true, as others were in hiding about the country, but it is evident that a good number were rounded up and taken to Aran.

Meanwhile, Sir Roebuck Lynch was declared a traitor, and one of the many London Adventurers, Erasmus Smith, took possession of the islands. His interest was later bought by Richard Butler, fifth son of James, first Duke of Ormonde. Richard became Earl of Aran in 1662. This title was conferred on Charles, brother of the second Duke of Ormonde in 1693, with whom it became extinct in 1758. It was revived in favour of Sir Arthur Gore, Bart, in 1762.

How Captain Robert Deey came to be captain of the Cromwellian garrison on Aran is a mystery, as he was an alderman of Dublin and a shoemaker by trade. His company, which held both Inishboffin and Aran, consisted of a lieutenant, an ensign, two sergeants, three corporals, two drummers and ninety men. With the Restoration the whole military establishment seems simply to have been transferred to the new regime, for Deey's appointment was reaffirmed by an order of 2 September 1662. He eventually went back to Dublin, where he was mayor in 1672.

The Ormond Papers give some indication of the needs of the island garrison. In August 1662 three months' pay was advanced to Captain Deey to buy winter provisions—beef, butter, oatmeal. Captain John Sanders, the second-in-command, put in demands for £30 for a new boat and £34 to repair the houses near the forts. Later it was reported that there was no evidence that he had, in fact, used the money for these works.

In February 1664 it was noted that Aran needed guns—'two long sakers or demisakers deficient which are needed to command the harbour as there are only five iron minions and two demi-culverins which are too faulty to clear the harbour'. It was decided that two guns lying on Galway strand might be sent out to Aran, and £150 was authorised to buy a frigate and do some building repairs. It was noted that bad weather might cause the boat crew (the link with the mainland) to be out for six to eight weeks at a time, and that with the present garrison of only twenty-eight men there were not enough to work the ship and hold the fort.

Major Bayley was the next commander. In January 1665 the Ormond Papers authorise delivery to him, for the troops in Aran and Inishboffin, sixty coats, breeches, stockings and shirts, and fifteen barrels of powder, forty great guns, 200 great shot, 100 swords, 200 muskets and two drums with sticks. Major Bayley seems to have been an unpleasant character, and John Allen in 1665 complained of the commander's attempt to force him to become a tenant of the Earl of Aran instead of the Countess of Mountrath. The Major defended himself with a long and specious explanation. In 1681 he appears again, having a cast of hawks sent from Aran to the Earl.

With the coming of William of Orange to the English throne, a garrison was sent to the islands after Galway surrendered in 1691, and seems, off and on, to have been maintained there for some time. Thus, when a Jacobite invasion of Scotland was rumoured in 1708, soldiers were sent to the islands. But times were much more peaceful, and the matter became yearly less urgent. The Ormond Papers of June 1710 record Sir Stephen Fox petitioning the Queen for bedding, etc, to lodge a company in the islands, his by purchase. He says that during the war with France the islands were often plundered and the houses destroyed by French privateers, who infested the coast every summer. The fort had been neglected in peacetime, but it should be refortified. Soldiers were quartered there in summer but withdrawn in winter, and, when they came back in the spring, they found their bedding, etc, 'spoiled and embezzled'. The garrison on Aran dwindled away as the islands ceased to be of strategic importance and passed into a long period of isolation, poverty and rack renting, from which they only began slowly to emerge with the setting up of the Irish Free State.

Inishmaan today is the most consistently Irish-speaking part of Ireland, where English really is (in 1971) a foreign language which not everyone speaks. The islanders are completely Irish and yet, to confound the proponents of racialism and racial inheritance, moulded in feature and blood group by the prolonged stay of the English garrisons.

Two important studies have, in fact, been made of the physical characteristics of the people of Ireland, and of the blood groups of the Aran islanders. The first is a massive publication that appeared in 1955, *The Physical Anthropology of Ireland*, by Ernest A. Hooton and C. Wesley Dupertuis. The second, published in 1958, is Earle Hackett and M. E. Folan's 'The ABO and RH Blood Groups of the Aran Islanders'. Nobody coming to the islands can fail to note that most Aran people are different from mainlanders, and that this is a matter of their build and not of their island clothes, which are falling more and more out of fashion. Hooton and Dupertuis stress the differences somewhat technically :

> It is thus apparent that the Arans are characterised by a population which is even more distinctive anthropometrically than geographically. The men of these islands diverge significantly from the run-of-the-mine Irish in nearly every metric and indicial feature. Tallness, long-headedness, chamaccephaly, leptoprosopy and linearity of body build are the outstanding characteristics of the men of Aran.
>
> Dark skins, straight hair, sparsity of beard and body hair, large brow ridges, low foreheads, high straight noses, and good teeth characterise the Aran islanders morphologically.

The research sample found the mean weight of an Aran man 1lb below the national average, his height 1cm above. They are extremely long-headed, and have the longest noses recorded in the Irish samples. The face is very long, with the depth coming in the lower jaw. The skin is quite often brown, the eye blue-brown or blue. Aran hair is mostly straight, curly varieties being rare, with the lowest proportion of really dark hair in all the Irish samples but the highest proportion of flat brown hair and red-brown hair, and only exceeded by Sligo men in the incidence of red hair. Slanting eyes were rarer than anywhere else in Ireland, and, another curious feature, 37 per cent of the Aran sample had not had their wisdom teeth through.

The authors concluded that the Aran people were the most inbred and homogeneous of all the Irish county samples they studied, and believed their physical characteristics had been affected by the presence of the garrison troops, who were hardly likely to have led celibate lives. This suggestion is borne out by Hackett and Folan's article on blood-group research. The authors claim that blood-group distribution patterns are very old, and that local variations can be tied in with known movements of people in the last 2,000 years. Invaders and settlers coming into Ireland raised the proportion of blood group A. The blood group ratios in Aran, ABO, differ markedly from the adjacent counties Clare and Galway, coming much closer to the proportions found in the eastern counties of Wicklow, Carlow and Wexford, and still nearer those of the north of England, where Saxon and Gael have probably mingled and intermarried for centuries. Again, the Rh factor occurs in different proportions to that of the adjacent mainland. The teeth of Aran children appear to resemble those of London children!

The people of Gorumna Island resembled those of Aran, but the people of Inishboffin, on which the soldiers were also stationed, have quite different physical characteristics. Aran, one suspects, had the larger influx of soldiers and officials, and the officials remained after the garrison went, and can be deduced from statistics on religious denominations in the islands—in 1861 there were ninety-five Protestants, quite a high proportion of 'outsiders' for a small island, but by 1926 there were only two.

The fact that blood group and physical characteristics seem to show a strong English admixture (and when the garrison was greatest, the islands' population was smaller than it would become later, so intermarriage would have a greater effect) is reinforced

83

by the evidence of personal names. The 1821 Census, the first taken, records a number of very English names—Barry, Billett, Boyle, Broughton, Carr, Cadsim, Coen, Gould, Hetherington, Jennings, Mollineaux, Nee, Nolly, Rochford, Simmers, Simpson, Taylor, Thompson, Wiggins, Wilson, and York. It will be recalled that it was old Mr Wiggins, said to be descended from a Cromwellian, who remembered Dun Mor as Dun Aengus. At Kilcananagh in Inishmaan nineteenth-century gravestones bearing the names Robinson and King can easily be found. The English or at least non-Connacht names of the 1821 Census have not all survived, however, and others have entered from Connacht. J. R. W. Goulden, who studied the Censuses in detail, found 135 surnames in the islands in 1821, which total had dropped to sixty-one in 1892, comprising forty-four from the earlier list and seventeen that were new. In 1951 there were seventy-five names, fifty-five persisting from 1892 and twenty that were new. The Hernons today believe that they descend from the garrison of Cromwellian times.

In reality the Aran islander is a big, powerful and often handsome man, or a woman of boldly moulded features and often the carriage of a queen. The modern islanders, with better feeding and perhaps more contacts and marriage with mainlanders, are taller than the men of fifty years ago. (An earlier survey of their characteristics was made in 1893 by A. C. Haddon and C. R. Browne.) But whatever their mixture of gene and blood group, they are as completely Irish in thought and speech as are to be found anywhere in the country.

6 LIFE ON THE ISLANDS IN THE NINETEENTH CENTURY

W HEN, in 1700, the eminent naturalist Edward Lhwyd visited the Aran Islands, he was perhaps the first of the long series of naturalists and antiquaries to arrive there. In Ireland the eighteenth century began with the full savagery of the penal laws against Catholics still in force, but it also saw the beginning of travel writing about the country, and the journeys of visitors seeking the curious, the unusual, the antique. Dr Johnson and Boswell went sailing about the Hebrides in 1773, and by that date there was considerable interest in such remote island corners of the earth, their monuments and the habits of the people who lived there. The nineteenth century saw the Aran Islands once more receiving attention from travellers and writers.

Throughout the eighteenth and nineteenth centuries the islands were still enjoying an equal or even higher standard of life than the adjacent mainland. The seas round them teemed with fish, and the potato famine could not, therefore, be quite so total a disaster as for people living inland. The Aran people were self-supporting farmer-fishermen, and might have lived quite well had it not been for the enormous amount of rent that was squeezed from them. Sir Roebuck Lynch, in 1642, had been coolly lifting his £400 a year, no small sum in those days, and during the early nineteenth century over £2,000 was being collected annually.

Meanwhile, the introduction of the potato to the western regions of both Ireland and Scotland allowed more and more people to live on less and less land. The potato supply for a whole year can be grown on much less an area of ground than a year's supply of oatmeal. If the potato crop fails, as it did in the Irish and Scottish potato famine years, the smallholders do not have enough land to turn to an alternative food plant, and any other 'cash crop' they may be able to produce is needed for the rent. The potato has been, rightly, described as an 'instrument of pauperisation'. Sir Walter Raleigh is frequently claimed as the person who introduced it to Ireland, where it was long regarded with distrust and only gradually came to be grown on a large scale. Probably the Aran Islanders started its cultivation sometime in the eighteenth century, and became increasingly dependent on it.

Once it had become part of island agriculture, island life settled to a pattern of farming and fishing that remained virtually unchanged for a couple of hundred years. J. M. Synge recorded such a way of life in the early 1900s, and one suspects that neither he nor any other visitors ever expected it to change as quickly as it eventually did. Much of the old way of life continued into the 1930s, when Robert Flaherty captured part of it in his documentary film *Man of Aran* (1934). In fact, the real improvement in island living conditions and really rapid change belongs to the period following World War II.

For Ireland in the early part of the nineteenth century, Samuel Lewis's *Topographical Dictionary* (1837) is a storehouse of invaluable information about the whole country and it seems worth quoting him on Aran, whose population was then 3,191 :

> The surface of all the islands is barren rock, interspersed with numerous verdant and fertile spots. There are many springs and rivulets, but these afford in dry weather a very inadequate supply of water, which is either brought from the mainland for the use of the cattle, or the cattle are removed thither during the continuance of the drought. The best soils are near the shore and are sandy, with a mixture of rich loam : the prevailing crops are potatoes, rye, and a small kind of black oats; the inhabitants raise also small quantities of barley and wheat, for which they apply an additional portion of seaweed, their only manure; and they grow small quantities of flax; but the produce of their harvests seldom exceeds what is required for their own

consumption. The pasture land is appropriated to sheep and goats, and a few cows and horses, for which they also reserve some meadow : the mutton is of fine flavour and superior quality; but the most profitable stock is their breed of calves, which are reputed to be the best in Ireland, and are much sought after by the Connaught graziers. The grasses are inter-mingled with a variety of medicinal and sweet herbs, amongst which the wild garlick is so abundant as to give a flavour to the butter. The plant called *Rineen* or 'fairy flax' is much relied on for its medicinal virtues in almost all cases; the tormentil root serves in place of bark for tanning; and there is another plant which gives a fine blue dye and is used in colour-ing the woollen cloth which the inhabitants manufacture for their own wear. The fisheries are a great source of profit, and in the whole employ about 120 boats; of these 30 or 40 have sails and are from five to ten tons burden; the rest are small row-boats and canoes or corachs. The spring and beginning of summer are the season for the spillard fishery; immense quanti-ties of cod, ling, haddock, turbot, gurnet, mackerel, glassin, bream and herring are taken here; and lobsters, crabs, cockles and mussels are also found in abundance. The inhabitants rely chiefly on the herring fishery, which is very productive; and in April and May, many of them are employed in spearing the sun fish or basking shark, from the liver of which they extract considerable quantities of oil. Hares and rabbits abound in these islands, which are also frequented by plovers, gannets, pigeons, ducks and other wild fowl; and the cliffs are the resort of numerous puffins, which are taken for the sake of their feathers by cragsmen, who descend the cliffs at night by means of a rope fastened round the body, and are lowered by four or five of their companions. In one of the islands a very fine stratum of dove coloured and black marble has been discovered; and from the various natural resources of this apparently barren district, the inhabitants are enabled to pay a rental of from £2,000 to £3,000 per annum to the proprietor.

When one recalls that £10,000 a year made Mr Darcy in Jane Austen's *Pride and Prejudice* (1813) a very rich man, one can understand how heavily that £2,000 to £3,000 a year pressed on the Aran islanders.

Even so, on Inishmore some 400 island children were attend-ing four 'pay schools' in 1837, for this was long before the days of free education. There was one Roman Catholic priest on the island, and he had to cross to the other two in order to celebrate mass and minister to the people there. Catholic emancipation had finally come in 1829, and Inishmore had a newly erected, slated chapel at Oghil. Killeany was still the main port and the Fishery Board had built a pier there in 1822. Kilronan has the better harbour facilities, and, when it acquired a pier also, began to grow at the expense of Killeany in the early 1840s.

There was a signal tower erected on the highest point of Inisheer but now a lighthouse and signal tower were constructed on the heights of Inishmore close to Dun Oghil. This lighthouse began to operate on 1 May 1818, and its substantial ruins still survive. It is described as 'exhibiting a bright revolving light from 21 reflectors, which attains its greatest magnitude every three minutes and may be seen from all points at a distance of 28 nautical miles in clear weather'. The *Parliamentary Gazetteer of Ireland* (1846) says the whole installation on Inishmore cost £880 18s 4d. Later on, the islands got two principal lighthouses, to define their whole length, one on Inisheer and the other on the Brannock Islands off the northern tip of Inishmore. These two lighthouses date from 1857, and to them was later added the light on Straw Island at the entrance to Kilronan harbour.

The old eighteenth-century signal tower on Inisheer is very like the sixteenth-century O'Briens' Castle, which is close beside it. Inisheer's skyline has the appearance of two castles as a result. The signal tower is weather-slated, slates being fixed to the walls like the scales of a fish, and preventing the driving rain working into the masonry underneath. Weather-slating was a common feature of old houses in county Cork, where slates were quarried in the local rocks.

Lewis says also that Inisheer was said to make the best kelp that reached the Galway market, and that the Inishmaan people were chiefly fishers and kelp-makers: 'they have a few row-boats and a number of canoes or corachs, made of osiers and covered with pitched canvas'.

The responsibility of the landlord, then a Mr Digby, toward

Page 89 Meeting the Galway boat at Kilronan: *(above)* c 1900. Island people as Synge knew them, in old style, homespun and homemade clothes; *(below)* today

Page 90 Inter-island traffic: the trawler, *Ros Ronain*, off Kilronan, carrying passengers and cargo to Inishmaan and Inisheer. Note building material and bottled gas. Curraghs are the more usual means

his tenants, these subsistence farmer-fishermen, is indicated in figures given by John T. O'Flaherty, writing in 1825. He says Mr Digby was one of the best of landlords, collecting £2,700 per annum from the islands in rental and out of this allowing 20 guineas to the school houses for the education of orphans and £20 for clothing the poor.

Ireland's first official census was taken in 1821, when there were 2,285 people living on Inishmore, 387 on Inishmaan and 421 on Inisheer. These numbers went up as time passed, but did not decline as violently as in other parts of the country during the disastrous Potato Famine. Thus the Aran Islands had 3,093 people in 1821, 3,521 in 1841, and 3,333 in 1851. The 1841 Census was the last before the famine, which began in 1845 and continued over the next few years, as there was then no method known of controlling potato blight. As is well known, the failure of government to take massive emergency action led to the death from starvation and starvation-caused disease of about 1,250,000 Irish people. About the same number emigrated, but many of them died at sea or on arrival in the New World. Islands stood the best chance of survival, for they had access to fish in the sea, shellfish, and seabirds and their eggs. In the Aran group Inishmore took the brunt of the famine, but suffered less acutely than the mainland. Mainlanders, in fact, looked across to these islands of comparative plenty and came sneaking across to them. Some of these refugees remained, but others, so modern island tradition says, were forced to go back at the behest of the landowners, who thought their presence would endanger the islanders' livelihood. Island memory is that some of those sent away could have stayed, instead of being forced to sail away to starve.

Some of the landless refugees who were able to stay 'made' land on contract under a two-year agreement, at the end of which period the land reverted to the owner. Most of the seaweed was already earmarked by existing farmers, but the refugees managed to scrape up some, together with baskets of clay from crevices in the rocks, and make their bit of land—which meant food for that year at least.

F

Canon John O'Hanlon, in a footnote to his account of one of the Aran saints in his unfinished but monumental *Lives of the Irish Saints* (1873), writes feelingly about this 'making' of land and tenant exploitation. Visiting St Brecan's church at Onaght, the Canon was 'shown a *gort* or small garden, by a peasant, who informed him that his grandfather brought seasand and seaweed in baskets from the seashore, which he laid on the naked rocks to form soil of a considerable depth. A good stone house was built by the tenant on the spot, and a wall enclosed the small tenement. For that poor homestead and plot—where not only were the improvements but the very soil created by the peasant's unaided toil—one pound annually was extracted as rent. No human ingenuity could procure much more than such a return, from the culture of that *gort*; and yet this was only a solitary instance of similar hard cases which fell under the writer's observation'.

Such conditions made it natural for Aranmen to be involved in the Land League agitations, and in occasional violence. Militant islanders walked the blindfolded cattle belonging to the landlord over the Dun Aengus cliff edge. And Pat Mullen recalled that his mother was among those women of Inishmore who once successfully stoned the sheriff and his men out of the island when they came to collect rent and evict tenants.

Inishmaan escaped such scenes for a long time because no islander would act as bailiff and point out the cattle of the person to be evicted. It was not, of course, merely a matter of not being able to pay the existing rent, but of continual demands for rent increases—or 'rack renting'.

However, when J. M. Synge was on Inishmaan, one islander did turn traitor, 'sold his honour', and, though twice a storm prevented the posse landing, they did ultimately arrive. Synge watched them, 'the boats being lowered, and the sunshine gleaming on the rifles and helmets of the constabulary who crowded into them'. He described how the police party visited each of the houses of those to be evicted, of the horror the islanders felt at the desecration of the hearth, the putting out of the fire and the blocking of the door with stones. The few animals the families owned were sought for and rounded up. One islander suggested loosing the bull on the invaders but Synge advised against this. In the event, this particular eviction was comparatively mild; some houses had excuses, and bargaining at the pier restored the beasts to their owners. 'It was plainly of no use to take them away, as they were worth nothing', Synge adds.

With this sort of background, it is possible to understand why Inishmore had such an unconscionable number of policemen in the 1880s, with agrarian unrest and demands of Home Rule abroad. Oliver Burke, writing in 1887, gives the islands' population as 3,118 Roman Catholics, 45 Protestants, with three Catholic churches and one Protestant, two priests, one parson, one doctor, four schools and teachers, and no less than three police barracks and 18 policemen.

During the heroic days of 1916 (the Easter Rising) and the struggle that led to the establishment of the Irish Free State, the Aran Islands were a backwater. However, they were able to give shelter and refreshment to some of the men actively engaged on the mainland, and so were the object of raids by the Crown forces and the hated Black and Tans. One islander, Lawrence McDonagh, was shot in 1920. His monument is on the roadside between Kilronan and Monaster Kieran. The Black and Tans, in a search over the island, met McDonagh on his way to mass, and told him to go home. He, thinking he would not miss mass, and given no other instruction but to go back off the main road, started off for church by the other, lower, road. While so doing, he was seen by the Tans, gunned down, and died a few days later.

A more rational land distribution and extensive owner occupation slowly developed in Ireland. It started with the work of the Congested Districts Board in 1891, when surveys were made of the condition of the overcrowded and desperately poor western countryside of Ireland. The Board began the policy of breaking up big estates and encouraging owner occupation. In the islands, they undertook construction work on Kilronan pier to improve the harbour facilities there, making it into the islands' principal port, as it still is.

In general, the islanders had a long-standing reputation for peaceful behaviour. The old accounts say they were long-lived, hard working, not given to drink or quarrelling. Oliver Burke (1887) quotes a letter from Philip Lyster, then magistrate of the district that included Aran :

> In the last century [ie the eighteenth] justice used to be admin-
> istered by one of the O'Flaherty family, the father of the late
> James O'Flaherty, of Kilmurvey House, Esq. J.P. He was the
> only magistrate in the islands, but ruled as a king. He issued his
> summons for 'the first fine day', and presided at a table in the
> open air. If any case deserved punishment, he would say to the
> defendant, speaking in Irish, 'I must transport you to Galway
> gaol for a month'. The defendant would beg hard not to be
> transported to Galway, promising good behaviour in future.
> If however, his worship thought the case serious, he would draw
> his committal warrant, hand it to the defendant, who would,
> without the intervention of police or anyone else, take the
> warrant, travel at his own expense to Galway and deliver him-
> self up, warrant in hand, at the county gaol.

Synge believed that the police were the cause of crime on islands like Aran. On Inishmaan, without police, a quarrel would blow over, but on Inishmore, where men were paid to intervene, a case would be brought and, if a conviction was secured, a family feud begin to develop, which might in due time even end in murder.

HOME AND FARM

The original Ordnance map shows that the Inishmore settlements were in clusters, not related, as when the road came later, to a linear pattern along the length of the island, but across it. A man's life lay between his fishing at the shore, his fields behind the shore, and his rough grazing on the 'back' of the island, over toward the high cliffs.

Island farms were and still are small and fields scattered. Nobody has or ever had all their fields in a single parcel of land.

The complex of stone walls encloses differently owned fields. Stones are even used for gates, two upright pillar stones or a well turned end of wall marking the entry, which is filled with more loosely built walling, easy to pull out and put up again. Today some more conventional gates are to be seen, but by and large Aranmen have long been in the habit of putting up and pulling down walls to enter and leave their little fields. Within, the soil is normally worked in the long spade-dug ridges called 'lazy beds' in spite of the amount of labour necessary. One feature of lazy-bed ridge cultivation is that it allows better weed control than do rows of vegetables all set on the flat.

The little fields produce potatoes, onions, carrots, lettuce, cabbage, hay and rye, and there are small enclosures growing willows for basket-making. In the old days, as already noted, oats and flax was also grown. Flax-growers feature in the 1821 Census, and in 1971 a very old man in Kilronan, Mr B. Gill, could recall that flax had been grown on Inishmore, 'up on the rocks', and that a special small wheel had been used for the spinning of it.

The stone walls surrounding the little fields form a maze in which a stranger can easily find himself in navigational difficulties. Boreens (lanes) and very narrow, one man wide 'roadeens' give access to many of the fields, others being reached by pulling down the stone 'gates'. Each farmer and his wife and family had (and still have) to do a good deal of walking to visit all their fields and tend the stock in each of them. On the waterless land on the 'back' of the island, where the cattle were pastured in winter, the man had to carry water daily to the animals. In summer the cattle were normally on the lower fields, near the house, and the woman did the watering while her man was out most of the day fishing. A twice-daily journey must also be made to do the milking, and then to carry milk or other feed to young calves which may be penned in yet other enclosures. The system of rain-collecting cisterns, adopted in the 1920s, has now reduced the amount of water-carrying that has to be done, but the other journeys must still be made.

Butter was made (and sometimes still is) in a wooden churn at home from the milk.

In 1917 Nurse Hedderman noted that the islanders' desire for a robust calf led them to let it suckle the cow much longer than mainland farmers normally considered necessary. Island calves were (and still are) well grown, robust animals, much sought after by mainland buyers. Getting them to the mainland represents a great deal of effort, for, at Inisheer and Inishmaan, where there is no suitable pier, they must be swum out to the ship behind a curragh and then hoisted aboard. Originally the animals went in sailing hookers, but now they travel by the Galway mailboat. Animals imported in to the islands had, and have, to undergo the reverse process. Surprisingly large animals can also be transported in curraghs, with their legs tied and padded to prevent their plunging through the thin canvas skin of the boat.

Pigs were reared on the islands until very recent times, when the increasingly high cost of feeding stuffs made it uneconomic. The piglets, or 'bonhams' as they are known in Ireland, were often bought on the mainland and shipped out to the islands. Mainlanders sometimes made very profitable sales, for the Aranmen might have to complete bargaining against the imminent departure of the *Dun Aengus* for the islands.

The whole difficult job of transhipping animals was repeated when it was necessary to send considerable numbers of donkeys, jennets and Connemara ponies in June to the mainland pastures, and bring them back in September. Synge says that this form of shipping presented even greater difficulties 'than that of the horned cattle. Most of them are wild Connemara ponies, and their great strength and timidity make them hard to handle on the narrow pier, while in the hooker itself it is not easy to get them safely on their feet in the small space that is available'. Horses did, in fact, receive some cuts from each other's hooves. 'Sometimes a large mare would come down sideways on the back of the other horses, and kick there till the hold seemed to be filled with a mass of struggling centaurs, for the men themselves often leap down to try and save the foals from injury.' In general, surprisingly little

96

harm was done to the animals. At that time there was but one bit and saddle on Inishmaan, and this was used by the priest on Sunday when he came in by curragh and rode up to the chapel to say mass.

Panniers on donkey back were used to carry seaweed and sand from the shore to the land for manuring and for the 'making' of new fields. Similar creels were carried on the backs of men and women with the same loads. There were also little two-wheeled carts, traps and jaunting cars, owned by the more affluent.

The very poor carried everything on their own shoulders. It seems likely that a man wishing to marry might first have to 'make' enough land to support his wife and the family he hoped to raise. The islanders cut the seaweed at low tide and carried it up to the fields or the places where land was to be 'made', as well as collecting that which was thrown ashore by the big storms.

The island houses were placed near springs and in the shelter of the hillside. The traditional house was long and low, one room 'deep'. Settlements on the islands today have a tendency to move downhill, as the new houses being built are much taller than the old and require greater shelter from the wind sweeping over the 'back' of the islands.

Cottages were and are thatched with rye straw grown on the islands. The thatch fits flush with the gable ends, leaving no overhang where the wind could tug a corner loose. The rye is harvested by being pulled up by the roots, the soil shaken off, and the stems tied into sheaves and stooked to dry. The grain, for next year's seeding, is threshed out by slashing the heads against a stone. In the old days straw ropes were made to lash the thatch to the roof.

Synge left an account of the making of the ropes:

Two men usually sit together at this work, one of them hammering the straw with a heavy block of wood, the other forming the rope, the main body of which is twisted by a boy or girl with a bent stick specially formed for this employment. In wet weather, when the work must be done indoors, the person who is twisting recedes gradually out of the door, across the lane, and sometimes across a field or two beyond it. A great length is needed to form the close network which is spread over the thatch, as each piece measures about fifty yards. When this work is in progress in half the cottages of the village, the road has a curious look, and one has to pick one's steps through a maze of twisting ropes that pass from the dark doorways on either side into the fields.

When the islanders had made several huge balls of straw rope, there was a kind of thatching party, in which a man's neighbours all rallied round in high spirits and great good humour to help him thatch his house. Straw Island (or, in Irish, Illaunatee, 'Island of the House') used to grow a lot of rye for thatching. In 1717 Edmund Fitzpatrick of Galway sublet Inisheer to Andrew French, also of Galway, for an annual rent of £100 and liberty to cut and carry as much straw from Straw Island as should be necessary for thatching all Inisheer's houses.

Straw rope could also be used to make articles of furniture : it was wound and stitched into the required form. With the coming of more money, easily available balls of twine replaced the straw rope to hold down island thatch. Today twine is itself being superseded, and the rye thatch on Synge's beloved Inishmaan is partly held in place by the colourful blue and orange of nylon cord. The use of man-made cord will give thatch a longer life, for the straw rope and twine decayed before the thatch itself.

Islanders still make baskets from willow rods. In the 1900s Synge recorded that the islanders made wooden vessels 'like tiny barrels' for houshold use. Of course, clothing was all made on the island, wool spun from island sheep being woven and made up. Again, this is now a thing of the past, though there are still tailors on the islands, and the men often wear the traditional 'bawneen' (tweed) suits with sleeveless jackets, and some of them make and wear the rawhide shoe or 'pampootie'. This is simply a piece of cowhide cut to fit one's foot and laced round with a bit of old fishing line (sometimes nylon line now), excellent for walking on the slippery limestone rocks and scaling the walls.

Synge knew the islands as almost self-supporting. The cottage he stayed in still stands on Inishmaan :

> The kitchen is full of beauty and distinction. The red dresses of the women who cluster round the fire on their stools give an air of almost Eastern richness, and the walls have been toned by the turf-smoke to a soft brown that blends with the grey earth-colour of the floor. Many sorts of fishing-tackle, and the nets and oil-skins of the men, are hung upon the walls or among the open rafters; and right overhead, under the thatch, there is a whole cowskin from which they make pampooties.
>
> Every article on these islands has an almost personal charac-ter, which gives this simple life, where all art is unknown, something of the artistic beauty of medieval life. The curraghs and spinning-wheels, the tiny wooden barrels that are still much used in place of earthenware, the home-made cradles, churns and baskets, are all full of individuality, and being made from materials that are common here, yet to some extent peculiar to the island, they seem to exist as a natural link between the people and the world that is about them.

Synge was told of fever in a house down the road, but the reality of living under these conditions, below the surface charm and beauty, does not seem to concern him. Nurse Hedderman struggled with confinements in poor cottages, 'water scarce as wine', where the dangers of infection and germs were not under-stood. With no light, and having to scramble over walls in the dark of a stormy night to reach her cases, she felt much less romantic about island life than Synge. She concluded her book :

> The responsibility of a district nurse in such a spot is truly great, and more exhausting than the heaviest hospital work; and it is difficult to leave the island for months at a time. It is so wild around the shore that frequently no doctor can venture to land. Therefore, however critical the case may be, the district nurse must face it alone and unaided and just do the best she can.

Island fuel was normally turf (peat) imported from Connemara in sailing hookers. On Inishmaan they used to edge in alongside the rocks, chaffering over the price with the islanders, and then unloading on to the rocks when a bargain was struck. But cowdung was also used, and the women spent a good deal of time gathering it, patting it into cakes and setting it to dry. If properly prepared, the fumes were not unpleasant. Even as late as 1956 people were burning cowdung rather than pay the high price that turf then cost.

In 1878 on Inishmaan T. J. Westropp saw two women 'grinding at the mill'—working a hand quern to grind a little corn, probably oatmeal, one suspects. For small amounts of grain grown on the island's small fields, the hand quern is quite a practical mill but its use had evidently died out in other remote corners of Ireland at that date to judge by Westropp's delight in seeing this ancient machine in use.

To survive, Aranmen and women had to be versatile, and Synge thought that much of their 'intelligence and charm' was due to this fact, for without division of labour one was allowed a full and varied development of personality. Such 'varied knowledge and skill necessitates a considerable activity of mind. Each man can speak two languages. He is a skilled fisherman, and can manage a curragh with extraordinary nerve and dexterity. He can farm simply, burn kelp, cut out pampooties, mend nets, build and thatch a house, and make a cradle or a coffin. His work changes with the seasons in a way that keeps him free from the dullness that comes to people who have always the same occupation. The danger of his life on the sea gives him the alertness of a primitive hunter, and the long nights he spends fishing in his curragh bring him of the emotions that are thought peculiar to men to have lived with the arts'.

The seaweed harvest was, and still is, important to the islands. The first call on the supply was for the manuring of the potato plots and other fields; the rest was eagerly collected and dried for making kelp. This was a laborious job. One ton of kelp required the gathering of 25 to 30 tons of wet seaweed, and might perhaps fetch £5, or less if the buyer said it was of poor quality. Or, again, he might reject it out of hand.

In the summer kilns were built along the shore and the dried seaweed was fired in them. As it began to melt, it was stirred vigorously with long iron rakes until the kelp ran into a solid molten mass. It was only toward the end of its long history of manufacture that the buyers and makers realised that a better product resulted from not stirring vigorously, and obtaining a powder instead of a hard mass.

The winking lights of the fires were a notable feature of Irish coastlines in the days of kelp-burning. Aran continued kelp manufacture long after it had ceased in most parts of the country, and it only died out in the years following World War II. It was very hard work for very little money, but as a modern Inishmaan man put it, 'It was the only thing we could do to get any money'.

Fishing from the islands was sometimes profitable, but the landless man who had specialised in fishing was then left penniless and destitute when a slump came. Emigration has been a feature of Aran just as much as from the rest of Ireland. It seems to have begun well before the great exodus of potato famine days, for Aranmen were leaving as early as 1822. The transatlantic liners at one time came into Galway, which made it very easy to reach them; later their sailings were all from Cobh in county Cork, necessitating a long journey across the south of Ireland from Aran.

A very common pattern for emigration was for one member of the family to travel to America first, and if he or she made good there to send passage money to other relations. Such an arrangement also helped the new emigrant to settle in and find work in his new country. Meanwhile, those left at home were helped by remittances sent by those who had made the journey. In the old days, of course, leaving for America was a final break, a final farewell to family, friends and country. Very few would have the opportunity ever to return.

As already noted, none of the islands were as badly hit by the potato famine as the mainland. But Inishmore's population declined steadily in the years following the famine, though the two smaller islands tended to hold their people. It is possible that Inisheer and Inishmaan had a primitive but fairly stable economy—small-scale fishing and farming—and this resulted in only small variations in their population, whereas Inishmore, the larger unit, had more opportunities for diversified activity and was, perhaps for that reason, more at the mercy of outside economic forces.

CURRAGHS

The ships in which Aranmen went to sea are a story in themselves. Galway Bay hookers, and their smaller sisters, the pookauns, were probably two of the best small sailing boats ever built for fishing. Very few now survive, and those that do are cherished by sailing enthusiasts. Black-bellied and brown-sailed, they sped through the water with grace and sweetness; though to face bad weather in them, while reasonably safe, would be a rough and wetting experience. They were in use in Kilronan, and the Connemara boats used to come across with loads of turf; in 1971 a survivor of the breed was still so doing.

With sufficient manpower, quite large boats may be launched and hauled up on a beach, but the ship that is interwoven with Aran life and history is the little curragh. You roll her on her side when you beach her, the water sluicing out, and three men, bending under her, can carry her, upside down like some fantastic beetle, to her parking lot, where she rests, still upside down, on stone supports above high-tide mark. The curragh is one of the most ancient of craft, and very much, in origin, a homemade boat. A skin or skins were stretched on a framework of wood and wicker (some British river coracles had very light frames and the boat was a small one-man tub-like craft) and the boat was made.

In ancient Ireland curraghs of various sizes seem to have been much in use, together with other types of boat. Large curraghs were capable of making extended voyages, though in the legend of Brendan's voyage St Ita tells him that he would only succeed in his adventure if he built a wooden ship and not use, as on his first attempt, one in whose construction blood had been shed. This suggests that the wooden ship was the better for really long journeys. But the curragh is so light, portable and seaworthy that she was and is an extremely useful and safe little boat. She will, if the crew know how to handle her, live in almost any sea, and can be lifted ashore and safely parked on the rockiest of islands. Today curraghs are the only type of boat owned and used by the Inisheer and Inishmaan people. Everything is imported into the islands in them, and exports are towed out to the big mail-boat in them.

One suspects that the curragh took on a new lease of life with the introduction of tar. Animal skins were expensive and difficult to repair, but now the frame could be covered with canvas (the Aran people used old flour bags) and waterproofed with a liberal coat of tar. A tear in the hull was repaired in the same way as a snag in a fabric aircraft, by doping on a patch. The curragh's 'dope' was hot tar, smoothed on traditionally with a glowing peat.

Curraghs vary from one part of the coast to another. Those from Aran and Kerry (where they are called *naomhogs*) are the finest in present use in Ireland.

The materials are now entirely changed from other days. Instead of using local wood, ribs tied with thong or withy and a cowskin cover or flour bags, the curragh builder on Inisheer today uses all imported woods, white spruce for the gunwale, copper nails to join the parts, and new canvas that comes in bales. The gunwale is shaped first; then the embryo boat is turned upside down and the main ribs and cross members fitted, to form an open-work frame over which the canvas is then stretched, secured and thoroughly tarred. The oars are long, narrow and bladeless, pivoting on a thole pin that passes through a hole in a wooden lug secured to the shaft of the oar. Modern curraghs have two to four rowers. The boat is keelless, and depends for her 'grip' in the water on the oars and on the ballast. Proper ballasting is vital for safety : beach boulders are carefully selected and arranged at each trip, or a bag of sand may be used. The big Aran curraghs would step a little mast, hoist a sail and run before the wind when conditions were favourable.

Today the outboard motor provides the power for long runs,

and, since the ship's 'grip' in the water is now moved to the rear, ballasting properly is even more important. Aranmen, sometimes with a strengthened transom, fit the outboard in the normal position in the stern, but Kerrymen sometimes fit it inboard, having a movable panel cut in the boat's hull amidships.

Aranmen still use the curragh for long runs—across to Doolin in county Clare from Inisheer and Inishmaan, or out to sea fishing all day. Curraghs are too small to allow of much movement, so the crew must more or less sit still all day; in the old days they sat it out fasting, or with a little bread.

Curraghs are one of the most delightful boats to travel in, riding more in the sea than upon it and lifting incredibly to wild seas. It is a wet exhilarating experience, in which the traveller meets the sea at close quarters and learns to meet it safely. Control is entirely in the hands of the rowers or the man at the outboard, since there is no rudder. The dangerous moments in bad weather are at embarkation and landing—seizing the lull in the waves to push out into deep water, and timing the run-in on to the strand.

Robert Flaherty in *Man of Aran* demonstrated just what kind of sea a curragh could live in. But the Aranmen, for the film's sake, went out in seas they would normally not have attempted, and in fact took very grave risks for the sake of the film. Pat Mullen, who was 'contact man' for the film-makers, writing in 1934, says that a curragh could and did live in the 40–50ft breakers that raced through Brannock Sound at the northern end of Inishmore. But these enormous seas were cut from the final film. 'Mr Flaherty thought that an audience looking at this scene on the screen could never take in the fact that it was a real happening, it was unbelievable.' The huge seas of *Man of Aran*, therefore, were not the greatest that the curragh men experienced while making the film. Each little township had its own beach and knew its special features. They could, therefore, judge the moments of danger or safety by watching how the seas broke on cliff or rock. Every beach had its own peculiar difficulties and dangers, and in making the film local crews had to be secured for each particular stretch of the coast.

104

Pat Mullen quotes the words of one expert curragh man of that date, who was nicknamed the 'Duke' :

> He had often told me that a curragh is the best boat of her size in the world—but of course she only goes as long as man-power lasts. In order to get her at her absolute best, when she could live where a seagull could hardly fly, the crew must be fearless, understand how to conserve their strength, never wasting one atom of energy and giving only just what is needed; but above all there must be absolute rhythm in thought and movement, as though the entire crew was controlled by one brain. Three men in a good curragh can and have outlived the most furious gales but such crews are rare.

Synge described some pretty rough curragh crossings. An Aran-man also explained to him how controlled fear—the ability to foresee possibilities and take action to avoid them—was the curragh crews' insurance. 'A man who is not afraid of the sea will soon be drownded, for he will be going out on a day he shouldn't. But we do be afraid of the sea, and we do only be drownded now and again.'

Oliver Burke wrote in 1887 that the Aran Islands had 130 curraghs, valued at £6 each. In 1971 a brand new three-man curragh cost £50, to which one, these days, would have to add the price of the outboard motor. With proper care a curragh has a long life—depending on what kind of landing place you happen to have, whether on sand, or on rock liable to snag the skin or break a rib. The home of the modern Aran curragh is the two smaller islands, as Inishmore, with its good harbour, has changed over to large trawlers and lobster boats for its fishing, and the mailboat from Galway and other sizeable craft can, of course, tie up at Kilronan pier.

FISHING

The traditional Irish islander or coast dweller was a farmer-fisherman, and some Aranmen are still combining the two vocations. The fortunes of island fishing have varied from com-

105

plete lack of markets to the profitability of the 1960s, with big boats making good catches. To the stranger the custom of fishing from cliffs 200ft high, which was much practised in the past, is probably the oddest feature of Aran fishing. The cliffs are so sheer that one can both cast a long weighted line into the sea from their summits and haul up the fish when caught; and there are plenty of fish to be had off these rocks.

Aran people could and do salt and dry some of the catch for their own winter use. It is worth knowing the method, because the results are very good. The fish is gutted and opened out flat; then salt is liberally rubbed over it, and into the bones, and the treated fish are packed into a barrel and left to lie in brine for some weeks. They are then put out to dry on stones or a roof, and, once dry, will keep indefinitely. Boiling in water, either with the potatoes, the traditional way, or on their own, results in a tangy meal of salted mackerel, haddock, rock fish, or whatever has been caught.

When Flaherty came to Aran to make *Man of Aran*, the basking shark (the *liomhan mor* or sunfish) had been back for some years in island waters, and he tried to reconstruct the old hunting of this fish for its oil. Pat Mullen found two rusty harpoons in an old house and another two in Kilronan; new ones were made to the old pattern, and the film-makers by trial and by what old men could tell them, set about learning how to harpoon a shark and relive island shark-hunting of 100 years before.

According to Pat Mullen, shark-hunting was profitable off the west coast of Ireland in the 1830s. They were pursued in five-man hookers. It was also possible, it is said, to take a shark by concerted curragh action and a harpoon with chain and rope attached to a shore boulder wedged in a pothole. The liver was worth from £35 to £50 in those days and might yield about 200 gallons of oil, which was used for domestic lighting and in lighthouses. When the sharks left the island waters, dogfish oil was used for the former.

The sunfish, however, seems to have been a rather uncertain

Page 107 Curraghs: *(above)* on the beach in summer, Inisheer. One boat is being carried back to its parking place. The Connemara hills in distance, and contrails from jets among the clouds overhead; *(below)* about to off-load from a steamer. Building materials, animals and fodder are usually landed in this way

Page 108 Shipping animals: *(left)* cow being hoisted from curragh; *(right)* horse being towed ashore

source of income and oil. In a lecture on Irish fishes given in 1839 by Dr Ball, the speaker held that shark-fishing was not commercially worthwhile, but forecast that it might become a sport, as it now is in Irish waters, including those of Aran :

> The pursuit of sunfish, if undertaken by gentlemen in their yachts, would add no contemptible item to the list of wild sports of the West [of Ireland]. Sunfish are struck with harpoons, and afterwards killed with lances; and the capture, from its gamboling, uncertainty, difficulty and danger, possesses the excitement which renders many sports attractive, but which excitement, applied to industry, may urge on the current rapidly for a while, but only to divert it from its proper channel, to run waste in riot when successful, or stagnate in the pool of despond when the reverse.

DEATH

'They're all gone now, and there isn't anything more the sea can do to me.' The words that Synge put in the mouth of Maurya in his play about life on Aran, *Riders to the Sea*, could come from any woman in almost any island in the world. Many Aranmen were drowned at sea, and their bodies washed up on mainland shores, painfully identified it might be through their clothing by their relatives. Some came to grief putting to sea after a bout of drinking on the mainland or the big island. Nurse Hedderman reasoned with one patient on the evils of drinking—Solon and the wisest philosophers had avoided it—and got the time-honoured reply : 'If Solon and all the preachers had lived long in Aran, they'd want a pint.'

The keening or dirge wailed by the women is still remembered on Aran, though not practised any more. Synge watched two island funerals, one of an old woman and the other of a young man. For the latter the keening was more personal and poignant than for the old woman, who had, as it were, reached the extreme of age to which a person could be expected to live. The women formed a kind of chorus, each taking her turn in the 'leading recitative', seeming, 'possessed for the moment with a profound ecstasy of grief, swaying to and fro and bending her forehead to the stone before her, whilst she called out to the dead with a perpetually recurring chant of sobs'. This took place in the graveyard.

Wood for a coffin had to be carefully acquired and kept till needed. Synge tells of one bereaved family having to borrow from a man who had 'had this [wood] for two years to bury his mother and she alive still'.

On Inishmore, there was the unusual custom of erecting roadside monuments—pillars of stones topped by a cross cut in stone, and with an inscription asking prayers for the souls of the persons so commemorated. It seems possible that this was a way of making a memorial closer to one's home, and perhaps to one's neighbour's prayers, than the graveyard where the body was actually interred. The earliest of Inishmore roadside memorials is said to date from 1709.

The roadside memorials and the old gravestones are all inscribed in English, but, if you walk across from the old slab tabletop tombs at Kilcananagh in Inishmaan to the new graveyard, you will find that the recent headstones there are nearly all in Irish. The use of English on carved monuments in an Irish-speaking district shows one form of anglicisation, now reversed. The new Irish headstones, in fact, return to the tradition fragmentarily preserved in the old inscribed stones of Killeany, of monumental inscription in the language of the people.

7   THE GAELIC TRADITION

O N the Aran Islands today one stands at the end of an unbroken tradition that goes back perhaps even to the days before the Celtic peoples came to Ireland. It is difficult for people today, conditioned to note-taking, taping and photography as the means of recording history as it happens, and to books, films and television for storytelling, to realise fully the power of oral tradition. It is hard to realise that it can be strong, accurate and long-lasting, the old men (the seanachies) repeating the stories, the histories, the romances, and the young men listening, repeating, and correcting their errors in the recitation, until they too should be old and handing on the spoken words to their children.

Two quotations may make these points clear. Daniel Corkery believed the oldest traditional tales might be pre-Celtic, and, writing in his book *The Fortunes of the Irish Language* in 1954, he said :

> There is something of continuity in those great mythological stories which are the fundamental glory of Irish literature, no one knowing how much of them the Gaels brought with them from the Continent, nor how much of them they found honoured here at their coming. Even yet, after fourteen hundred years of Christianity, the folk-tale, the heroic poem, recited of a night-time by a Connemara or Donegal or Kerry *seanchaí* to his neighbours may be filled with such heroic names as the boy Patrick might have caught while he sat resting after the day's work with his fellow-labourers at an Antrim fireside —names like Dana, the Dagda, Angus Og, Manannan Mac Lir.

Pat Mullen, writing in 1934 and looking back to his childhood, describes this sort of storytelling on Inishmore in Aran :

Folklore tales would be told as we sat around our winter fire, tales of our grandfathers and great-grandfathers, of how they went to fairs on the mainland, how they played cards and fought, of how they danced and drank their jugs of punch. . . . The men of Aran in those days read little fiction. They lived in their stories, and their eyes flashed with fire or grew dim with emotion as a tale reached great heights of courage or sank down to sadness.

The Sons of Usna and Cuchulain, these heroes too came in and performed their deeds of valour and chivalry as we sat by our winter fire.

FOLKLORE, CUSTOM AND SUPERSTITION

Although a story of the Fianna, for instance, in the mouth of a good traditional storyteller can still be an exciting experience to listen to, folk stories generally are not to modern tastes and the seanachies are a rapidly dying race. The fulness of the traditions and stories they knew are, happily, preserved in the archives of the Irish Folklore Commission in Dublin, but only published in part as yet. Aran, like everywhere else, is switching to the more cosmopolitan culture and amusement represented by the printed page, radio, and television. Something, of course, remains on the ground; the localisation of many of the stories has left placenames —the use of the names 'Dermot and Grania's bed' for the Megalithic tombs, for example; and the Aer Arann pilot coming in low over Lough Inchiquin and recalling the story of the children of Lir, changed into swans, and localised there. 'Look', says he, 'there are swans on the lake today too.' If Corkery is right, here is a story perhaps older than the Gaelic people's coming to Ireland being told again in an aircraft en route to Aran.

The stories the Aran people listened to ranged widely. There were the great ancient story cycles about Cu Chulainn, and Fion and the Fianna, whose deeds were sung by the poet Oisin (Ossian). Then there were the stories of the saints and their deeds on the islands, and others about island history. The raid of Grace O'Malley was remembered, as was the great flood that swept across the low waist of Inishmore about 1640. The Rev Kilbride thought human bones revealed under the blown sand at the clochans of Eararna might be those of the crew of a French or Spanish ship which island tradition spoke of and claimed to have been wrecked there. The ship must have been sunk 100 or 150 years before the clochans were discovered in the 1860s.

There were stories to explain curious features of the islands. Aranmen knew that the ice-borne Connemara rocks did not belong to the islands, so a story was told of two giants, one who lived in the limestone area at Black Head and the other amongst the granites at Slyne Head, who would rouse themselves from sleep every seven years and start a furious quarrel, in their rage hurling at each other great blocks of stone that sometimes fell short on the Aran Islands.

Other stories concerned island people—gossip about contemporaries and near-contemporaries becoming more heroic in tone the farther they went back into history.

This kind of yarning went on not only round the household fireside, but among the men who sat up all night tending the kelp fires. Tom O'Flaherty, writing in 1934, tells how, as a young boy, he went along to the kelp-burning and 'listened eagerly to the conversation of the men. They talked of olden times and of the great kilns of kelp they burned, of going to Kilkerrin on the mainland to sell it and the adventures they had. That was the way with Aran islanders. They had appropriate stories for every season of the year. In the mackerel season they told stories of great hauls of mackerel and the dangers they encountered taking the nets, the prices they got for the fish and their fights with the buyers. It was the same way when they were engaged manuring, planting or digging potatoes, killing rock birds in the high cliffs on the south side of the island, thatching the houses or going down the cliffs for wreck'.

Of course, this kind of talk still goes on in pub or by the fireside, but now visitors often add their own contribution, swopping story for story. The stranger's story has always been a part of island life everywhere, illuminating another region of the world and another style of living.

The traditional stories of the seanachies also included what we could call 'novels', based on plots of international provenance. Synge picked up one of these and told it again in his book on the islands. The story might be localised in Ireland, and the characters given Irish names, but its point is universal—a foolish husband believes his wife has been unfaithful to him and tries to kill her; but she escapes, then reappears and rescues him by pointing out that no blood could be taken when a creditor demands his pound of flesh. Synge wrote :

> It gave me a strange feeling of wonder to hear this illiterate native of a wet rock in the Atlantic telling a story that is so full of European associations. The incident of the faithful wife takes us beyond Cymbeline to the sunshine on the Arna, and the gay company who went out from Florence to tell narratives of love. It takes us again to the low vineyards of Wurtzburgh on the Main, where the same tale was told in the middle ages, of the 'Two Merchants and the Faithful Wife or Ruprecht von Wurtzburg'. The other portion, dealing with the pound of flesh, has a still wider distribution, reaching from Persia and Egypt to the *Gesta Romanorum*, and the *Pecorone* of Ser Giovannia, a Florentine notary.

Aran even forestalled part of *Alice in Wonderland*, for Synge met a man on Inishmaan who, going rabbiting, declared he saw a rabbit 'sitting up by the wall with a sort of flute in its mouth, and it playing on it with its two fingers'. Perhaps island tongues were in cheeks when they told Synge this story. He had been playing on his fiddle and they dancing, and the talk had turned to the hearing of fairy music when the rabbit story was produced.

Belief in fairies was in Synge's time and later very real, universal, and sometimes dangerous. On the Irish mainland ghosts and fairies have had to beat a retreat before the advancing poles of the Electricity Supply Board. Powerful lights in house, cowstall, farmyard and township have removed the mystery from rustling leaves, scampering animals, dark shadows. But it is still very dark on the Aran Islands of an evening, for there is no street lighting (1971), though homes are well lit. When homes were dimly lit and the islanders very isolated, very alone, it was easy to believe in ghosts and fairies. Like some mainland people, some islanders still believe in ghosts and even fairies, and, it must be admitted, some ghost stories do seem to demand explanation. Synge recorded many island stories about the fairies. One islander confided the secret of protecting oneself from fairy attack—'take a sharp needle and stick it in under the collar of your coat and not one of them will be able to have power on you'.

For Nurse Hedderman, a few years later, belief in fairies was a horrible reality. It was thought in Aran and elsewhere that fairies could and did steal children and replace them with changelings. In fact, Aran boys wore petticoats like their sisters, to deceive the fairies, until they were quite grown up. Nurse Hedderman had to fight this belief, for a sick child might change so much in appearance and personality that the parents would become convinced it was a changeling and be unwilling to nurse it. One such 'changeling', sick with whooping cough, recovered, and then the mother claimed that the fairies had restored the original child to her again. The nurse found the men more receptive to modern ideas than the women, and the poorer people less superstitious than the better off.

Disease strikes so finally in an isolated community, normally far from help, that there is a great temptation to believe in curses, fairy interventions and the evil eye. 'No, he's not ill', they would tell the nurse, 'he's been overlooked' (by someone with the evil eye). To ward off this danger one gives the traditional greetings, which are blessings, and does not stand idly by when work is going on. It is unlucky to watch someone churning butter without yourself helping, even a little. In such circumstances the islanders used magical cures and folk remedies, which Nurse Hedderman strove, usually in vain, to prevent. The traditional cure would be tried first, and she would only be called in when it failed. Besides, it was thought the presence of a doctor or nurse would undo any good a local spell or charm could do.

The nurse, of course, was much involved with beliefs associated with marriage and childbirth. It was lucky to get a cast-off secondhand cradle for the first-born child; but unlucky for the mother to sew its first garments, which should come from a distance. The oldest rags were the safest to use, more resistant to the supernatural. A large needle was put in the baby's wrappings against the evil eye—recalling the advice given to Synge for dealing with fairies. Immediately after birth, butter mixed with some other substance was put in the mother's mouth as a protection against spells. The first person to come in after the birth must spit on the child, the mother and attendants, for luck.

The eve of May Day was a time when the fairies were supposed to be specially active and dangerous, and that night the cows were protected by being plastered with crosses of dung. May Day, Midsummer and Hallow-e'en (in autumn) are, of course, all critical times according to folklore. At Midsummer, on St John's Eve as it grows dark, the big St John's fires still blaze and the crowds gather round them. In 1971 the fires, however, were for fun, like those of the English Guy Fawkes night, and no longer of vital importance in human and animal welfare, as in the days when one was supposed to take home a coal from the bonfire to ensure good luck for the year. 'I knew it would be like this; he did not take in a red coal from the fire on St John's night', the nurse was told of a man with a septic finger. The Midsummer fires go back to pagan antiquity, a custom adapted to Christian use and a Christian feast day.

The pilgrimages, holy wells and the old crosses and churches played a very important part in old-style island life. Prayer was often the only possible hope in cases of illness that today would be whisked off to hospital and rapidly cured. As well as praying rounds at the island shrines, and making the big round of the whole island of Inishmore on Holy Thursday and Good Friday (20 miles, barefoot, with seven Paters, Aves and Glorias at each church on the route), the islanders used to go across to pray at St Brigid's well, inland from the cliffs of Moher in county Clare. The overnight vigil, the 'sleeping in the bed of the saint', took place not only at St Brecan's church at Onaght but at that of the Four Beauties, at St Kennerg's grave on Inishmaan, and at St Cavan's on Inisheer. While the idea of the vigil is very Christian, the 'sleeping in the bed' may be much older, for devotees of the Greek god of healing, Asklepios (Aesculapius), used to go and sleep in his temples to be cured in their dreams.

Nathaniel Colgan, a botanist who was studying the island flora in May 1892, encountered another widespread superstition —that evil, a synonym for disease, could be transferred from one person to another by the action of a witch or sorcerer. He was being watched by a group of islanders as he searched through the grass at Killeany for the Milk Vetch. Eventually one islander said: 'That's a very dangerous thing you're about; I've known a man killed that way'; he went on to tell of a friend called Flanagan who was dying at Oghil. In the last resort a *cailleach*, a wise old woman, was called in from Onaght, and just like the botanist, she had gone down on her hands and knees, plucked a herb and looked at the road—the first person she saw there (who in this case was an O'Flaherty) would take the disease of the sick person and die within twenty-four hours. Three or four of the younger men in the group watching Colgan scoffed at the story, but its teller insisted that Flanagan had lived and O'Flaherty had died.

Synge would amuse his hosts with simple conjuring tricks, and one old woman said to him:—'Tell us now, didn't you learn those things from the witches that do be out in the country?' Synge wrote:

> My intercourse with these people has made me realise that miracles must abound wherever the new conception of law is not understood. On these islands alone miracles enough happen every year to equip a divine emissary. Rye is turned into oats, storms are raised to keep evictors from the shore, cows that are isolated on lonely rocks bring forth calves, and other things of the same kind are common. The wonder is a rare expected event, like the thunderstorm or the rainbow, except that it is a little rarer and a little more wonderful.

The islanders were critical of him in their own way. Synge had a trick of cutting and rejoining a piece of string, and once, after the company had expressed due amazement, one of them faced him out. 'You can't join a string, don't be saying it. I don't know what way you're after fooling us, but you didn't join that string, not a bit of you.'

Nurse Hedderman was sent a gramophone on Inishmaan, the first that was ever there, and speaks rather movingly of the meeting of the old world of wonders and the new world of science. None of the islanders knew how to assemble the machine, but a visiting Oxford graduate came to their rescue and put it together. When the sound came on, everyone kept saying, 'somewhere there must be a person or there could not be a voice', as they crowded round to listen. The gramophone was therapeutic as well as entertaining:

> A woman who had been ill with nervous trouble for many weeks previously, heard of the mysterious music. She asked me to let her hear it. Of course I consented. It acted like a charm. The spell was instantaneous. She, too, forgot her trouble, and the sad, worn face, on which suffering had left its mark, at once lighted up with hope and pleasure. Often afterwards I invited her to come and hear the music, and her visits were invariably followed by happy results.
>
> I had no idea before that the islanders had such a passion for music and song. One evening all the old men had assembled at one of the cottages. Among the records was a hornpipe. Directly the first beat was played, six of the men stood up in a line, some distance apart from each other; all somehow procured short sticks, and at the first note, feet, arms and sticks commenced to keep time, each fellow swaying his body first to the right and then to the left. Scarcely any noise was heard, as they can move quite silently on the pampooties or cowhide shoes which they wear, the quiet being broken only by the clanking sound of the sticks as they clashed.

In the old days the islanders used to meet for social evenings in each other's houses and there would be singing and dancing. As elsewhere in Ireland, there was also the summertime, outdoor cross-roads dancing.

HY BRASIL

The vision of Hy Brasil, the mythical island to the west of Ireland, is a part of Aran folklore. There are several possible explanations for the myth. With luck, anyone getting the right concatenation of cloud and light, and perhaps mirage, may see the phenomenon that looks like an island far out to sea. Another explanation lies with the Irish *corpus* of voyage romances, in which the hero or the saint goes on a journey of adventure and discovery, visiting a series of wondrous islands. Where Chaucer used a pilgrimage to string stories together, this old Irish story form used a sea voyage. But there were also the very real voyages of Irish monks and of Vikings. St Brendan really did set sail, reaching as far as the Scottish islands in the sixth century and, rather later, Irish monks established themselves first on the Faroe islands, and then on Iceland, where they would have some experience of volcanic activity. After the Northmen made their permanent settlements on Iceland (from about AD 870), explorers ventured still further to the west. At the end of the tenth century Eric the Red led a party of settlers to Greenland, which had, in fact, been sighted by earlier Scandinavian sailors, and his son Leif went on to prospect the North American coast, evidence of which Viking arrival has now been found by archaeologists.

Of all the Irish voyage romances, Brendan's was by far the best known and most popular. It seems to have been written in the tenth century by an Irishman living on the Continent, long after the saint's death. The author drew on all sorts of source material —European legend and history and, one suspects, the stories being told by those energetic globe-trotters, the Icelanders. From them he probably took the story of what an undersea eruption is like—the story of the island of demon smiths exactly fits the reality, as Icelandic geologists discovered when they ventured ashore, early in 1964, on the new volcanic island of Surtsey in its early and violent phase. The crystal island story is about an ice floe or iceberg—these sometimes come into Icelandic fiords in a cold winter, and, of course, are well known to anyone sailing to Greenland. Brendan's voyage became a medieval bestseller, translated into a great number of languages, and may have influenced Dante's *Divine Comedy*.

It is also possible, if not highly probable, that Brendan's voyage and the other stories of land to the west influenced Columbus's decision to sail across the Atlantic. He, it seems, came into Galway, on his setting out, and sailed off ultimately out of the bay and past the Aran Islands.

There was yet another element in the early voyages—the legend of the Islands of the Blest, of the ever young, *Tir nan Oig*, and that somewhere part of the garden of Eden yet remained, to be discovered by a bold saint who dared to face the seas and search their high ridges and deep furrows. Such men indeed, some legends told, had made that landfall, and come back with flowers of paradise in their hands.

Land to the west—the mapmakers were sure of it, even if uncertain of its shape and position—and so all the old Atlantic charts have Brendan's Isle and/or Hy Brasil on them. Both islands appear on Ortelius's map of 1570. Mercator (1587) has St Brendan's isle west of Kerry. In 1655 a Dutch map put Hy Brasil at the Porcupine Bank, and Moses Pitt (1680) placed it south-west of Ireland. Brendan's Isle disappears from the charts in 1700, but Hy Brasil survived till 1865. The origin of the name *Brasil* is disputed, but the *Hy* is Norse and means an island.

Anyone with luck may see the meteorological phenomenon that people on Aran pointed to and called Hy Brasil. T. J. Westropp saw it several times, from Kilkee in county Clare between 1872 and 1896, and again from county Mayo in 1910. Art O'Lann-daigh, so called 'King of Aran', saw it in 1923 from Aran, and his description in Irish was published much later in the *Irish Press* of 8 November 1944. Westropp's account, that of a trained observer and historian, is worth quoting :

From the Diamond Rocks, Kilkee, I saw, more than once, between 1872 and 1896, the phantom island to which, from the influence of the medieval maps from 1325 downwards, the name of Brazil, or Hy-Breasail, was attached.
It appeared immediately after sunset, like a dark island far out to sea, but not on the horizon. On the last occasion I made

a rough, coloured sketch next day which shows the appearance as having two mountains, one wooded, in the low central tract; between rose buildings, towers and curls of smoke, rising against the golden sky westward.

I have on several occasions since then seen mirages of islands, but never have seen anything so matter-of-fact as the former 'vision of the lost Atlantis'.

THE INFLUENCE OF THE TRADITION

Of the many people who have been profoundly influenced by contact with the Aran Islands, the playwright John M. Synge (1871–1909) is the best known. His immersion in the life of Inishmaan influenced his writing and thinking profoundly. Robert J. Flaherty, 'father of the documentary', was never so deeply involved with Aran, yet the film *Man of Aran*, made between 1932 and 1934 on Inishmore, shows the same vision of a remote Irish-speaking and self-contained Celtic community on the Atlantic's edge as *Riders to the Sea*.

After the Famine years, Irish ceased to be the language of large areas of mainland Ireland, and by the time the Gaelic League and a revival of interest in things Celtic appeared, it was too late to restore it as the language of ordinary Irish people. So areas where Irish was still the first and often the only language, and where a full traditional Gaelic way of life flourished, assumed enormous importance to Irish nationalists and enthusiasts for the language.

The Aran group and the Blaskets were two of these areas. Both spoke very good Irish, both retained a full and rich Gaelic tradition and culture, and both accordingly attracted students, scholars and Celtic enthusiasts in considerable numbers. The Blasket Islands were ultimately abandoned but Aran continues to exist, though, as already noted, with a continuing loss of traditional storytelling and of the 'primitive' way of life that was once so much admired. Curiously, two other Irish-speaking islands, interesting and attractive in their own way—Tory in county Donegal and Cape Clear in county Cork—have never received anything like the attention that has been given to Aran and the Blaskets.

The Aran Islands have deeply influenced many people, scholars and writers as well as those who come to learn or perfect their knowledge of Irish and encounter a traditional Gaelic way of life. But the nature of this encounter has changed very considerably of late. The beautifully spoken Irish is still there, but the subsistence farmer-fisherman existence has given place to one in which the standards, the tools, and the equipment of daily life approximates increasingly closely to those of the mainland.

8   IN THE ISLANDS TODAY

ISLAND people who emigrated in their teens and only came back recently in old age to enjoy retirement at home are those most aware of the enormous changes that have taken place in Aran. The world they returned to is not the world they left, even if many of the familiar landmarks—curragh, pampootie, ass and cart—are still there. The old people who have lived through the transformation notice it less.

There is a marked difference between the three Islands. Inishmore, the largest, has much more of a mainland atmosphere than the other two. As already remarked, it has been more vulnerable to depopulation and more susceptible to changing economic conditions. It still is, for it is the island that must attract the most development, in tourism, in new industries, in fishing, and it will take the brunt of any failure.

Kilronan seems a little metropolis, with pier, harbour, guards barracks (police station), doctor, lifeboat, and the airfield just across the bay. Strung out along the length of Inishmore, each hamlet tends to have its own characteristics. It is an island of little settlements, whereas the other two seem each to form a single and integrated community of their own, though each is divided into 'villages' with their own names. Inisheer has a peculiar sweetness of character, and one that attracts many annually returning visitors. Inishmaan is the most Irish in speech and feeling, where a monoglot English speaker is definitely a foreigner and may need an interpreter to talk to a monoglot Irish-speaking islander.

COMMUNICATIONS

There are two verbal niceties about visiting the islands. Aran is always a singular name—one may not speak of the 'Arans'—and it is correct, and this applies to some other Irish offshore islands, to speak of going *into* them, ie not 'to the Arans' but 'into the Aran islands'.

The paddle-steamer *Citie of the Tribes* was, as already remarked, the ship that initiated regular passenger and cargo sailings from Galway to the islands. She was soon replaced by the little steamer *Dun Aengus*, a sturdy little Dublin-built vessel that carried the bulk of island cargoes for the best part of fifty years. She was operated by the Galway Bay Steamship Company, and when this was taken over by the Irish national transport system CIE (Coras Iompair Eireann) in 1951, she became the oldest steamer in regular service to be owned by any railway in western Europe. (CIE operates both trains and buses in Ireland.)

Citie of the Tribes was operated by the Galway company from February 1891 until 1903, when she was sold. The company had had another steamer, in addition to the *Dun Aengus*, and that was the *Duras*, built specially for them in 1892. When *Dun Aengus* was finally broken up in 1958, she had been forty-six years in service. Her adventures in the often wild seas of Galway Bay included going aground in 1947 on Inisheer after loading passengers and cattle from that island on a stormy day. The live cargo was disembarked successfully, but for some time it was thought the ship would be a total loss. However, she was refloated, repaired and continued her trek back and forth from Galway to the islands in all weathers. Dara Beag, a poet of Inishmaan, wrote an Irish song to commemorate her near shipwreck.

Dun Aengus was replaced by the larger MV *Naomh Eanna*, built in the same yard as the older vessel, and regarded by the island people as a much more official formal kind of ship than *Dun Aengus*. The latter's crew seem to have been 'part of the family' of the islands. Sailing would be delayed if some passenger

124

Page 125 (above) The priest arrives from Inisheer to say the Sunday mass on Inishmaan, 1971. One priest does duty for both islands and makes this curragh crossing each Sunday, weather permitting; (below) island backs after Sunday mass on Inishmaan. Here many of the women still wear the traditional dress and shawl

Page 126 The land: *(above)* driving donkeys along a boreen (lane) near Kilronan; *(below)* harvesting rye on Inisheer for thatching. The rye is pulled up by the roots, not cut

known to be travelling had not yet turned up; crew members would take 'messages' for you to Galway shops and bring them back. *Naomh Eanna* is also less handy for loading cattle off the two small islands.

She is the official mailboat as well as the regular passenger and cattle ship. She sails to the islands several times each week, depending on the season and the weather, tying up at Kilronan pier but transhipping to curraghs off Inisheer and Inishmaan. In summer the MS *Galway Bay* runs daily into Inishmore, augmenting the mailboat service and normally bringing a large crowd of day visitors. When *Naomh Eanna* is laid up for her annual overhaul, *Galway Bay* takes her place, but sails only to Kilronan. Supplies and passengers for the other two islands are then carried from Kilronan pier by a local fishing boat.

The Inisheer people frequently voyage to Doolin on the Clare coast by curragh, and it is normally fairly easy to get to Inisheer by one of their boats. Again, boats come and go from Inishmore to the Connemara coast, to the north in county Galway. Between the islands one may travel by the regular mailboat on her round, or by a local curragh or fishing boat. Island people also visit Galway on occasion on friendly Inishmore trawlers.

In August 1970 Aer Arann (Air Aran) began operating to the new airfield at Killeany with a ten-seater Britten-Norman 'Islander' aircraft, EI-AUL. The service was an immediate success, operating from a grass field near Galway city, and, later, from Shannon international airport as well. The aircraft flies a daily schedule, the number of flights varying with the number of passengers. It flies low, and gives in fine weather a tremendous view of the islands, the mainland of Connemara and Burren, the pilot pointing out places of interest to the passengers. Flying time from either Galway or Shannon to the islands is only 20 min as against the mailboat's 3 hr.

The island runways are levelled sand dunes sown with grass, which makes a hard dry sward. The Killeany runways are 1,700 and 900ft long, the main one running approximately south-east

H

and north-west, and the short one north-north-east and south-south-west. The Inishmaan strip was completed in 1971, a landing craft being used to carry heavy equipment into the island. Its two runways, which come into service in 1973, are south-east to north-west (2,200ft) and north-east to south-west (1,800ft). These island airfields are simply grass landing strips without any airport facilities or supplies of aviation fuel or oil. They may be used by visiting light aircraft that have been given permission to land by Aer Arann. The mail continues to be carried by boat, but the aeroplane brings out the day's newspapers.

Much recent work has been done on improving piers and roads in the islands. Kilronan pier recently was again extended, and the harbour is now adequate for the fishing boats based there. The other islands have small jettys and slipways; a small boat can tie up in safety for a short period at Inisheer pier, but it is not a permanent mooring.

Island roads were originally dirt tracks, as they still are on the two smaller islands. The principal road, running the length of Inishmore, has now been tarred, though the surface is kept deliberately rather rough for the benefit of the many ponies and traps still in use. The parish priest of Inishmore was the first person to own a car on the island—in 1959. Then one of the Guards (police) got one. By 1971 Inishmore had some thirty cars and many motorcycles, as well as some tractors and trailers and minibuses. The two smaller islands have a couple of tractors each, and Inishmaan has a minibus, but private cars are not worth-while as the distances are too short. Car and tractor ownership in the islands involves problems the mainlander hardly thinks about. There are no island filling stations, so one must import fuel in barrels. For maintenance, a car must go by mailboat to a mainland garage; and if the owner is able to do his own repairs and servicing, he still has the freight charge on parts brought out by the boat to the islands.

Two-wheeled carts, and even panniers on donkey back, are still used on the islands and on the little farms. The jaunting cars and pony traps on Inishmore meet the Galway boat and take visitors on sightseeing trips, as well as carrying their owners on their ordinary journeys about the island.

The mail from Galway arrives twice a week, weather permitting. Inishmore has two sub post-offices—Kilronan, and Kilmurvey. The latter opened in 1950, but the Department of Posts and Telegraphs (An Roinn Poist agus Telegrafa) think that the Kilronan post-office and money-order office date back to about 1897, when the Irish sub post-office network was established. They think that the two sub-offices on the two smaller islands were also founded at about the same time.

The old eighteenth-century signal tower on Inisheer must have been the islands' earliest direct link with the mainland. All three islands are now linked by telephone, and Galway may be dialled direct for the price of a local call. The telegraph service came to Kilronan on Inishmore about 1902, linked to the mainland by a submarine cable. In the early 1920s a call office and telephone exchange were added.

The submarine cable goes straight across from Inishmore to the mainland at Inverin in Connemara (county Galway). The system has been steadily enlarged and improved. First, two carrier circuits were added to the submarine cable, and on 9 October 1967 a single-channel radio link to Galway increased the number of circuits to four. On 12 August 1971 the two carrier circuits to Inverin were taken out of service and replaced by a twelve-channel radio link between Kilronan and Inverin. Kilronan now (1971) has eleven direct circuits to Galway; both the single-channel radio link to Galway and the submarine cable to Inverin remain in use.

Inisheer call office opened for service on 11 April 1954 and its telephone exchange on 9 June 1961. Inishmaan's call office opened at the same date, but its telephone exchange arrived earlier, on 17 August 1960. Until 24 July 1970 this telephone link between Inisheer and Inishmaan was carried by single-channel radio links to Ballinalocker on the Clare coast and then by wire lines to Lisdoonvarna exchange (county Clare). This arrangement ended on 24 July 1970, and was replaced by single-channel radio links to Tonabrookey (outside Galway city), the circuits being extended therefrom to Galway automatic exchange by underground cable.

On 2 July 1971 Kilronan (Inishmore) had forty-four working exchange lines, Inisheer three and Inishmaan four.

FARMING AND FISHING

Cattle continue to be the mainstay of island farming. These well grown healthy animals, mostly shorthorns, still command good prices. It was estimated in 1971 that some 600 or 700 cattle are sold off the three islands from January to May. The buyers come to the islands now in contrast to the old system whereby the owners took their beasts to mainland sales. A curious feature of the contemporary island economy is that though the buyer comes to the islands, makes the bargain there and pays the price, the owner must still pay the freight on the beast to Galway. This freight charge together with the customary 'luck money' (the return of a pound or so to the buyer) seems a hard burden on subsistence island farming. In Inisheer and Inishmaan it is necessary to swim the animals out behind curraghs to the ship, and more money is possibly involved in treating one's assistants at this job in the pub afterwards.

Cattle, a small number of sheep (some of which have dark brown or black fleeces), ponies, donkeys, goats, chickens, and the usual domestic cats and dogs make up the islands' livestock. There is no Creamery collection of milk as on the mainland, and butter is therefore sometimes made in a churn at home. The fields are too small and rocky for the most part for machinery to work in them, and most operations are still carried out by traditional methods—spade-digging into lazy-bed ridges, and scything grass and oats. Rye, grown for thatching, is not cut but pulled up by the roots to give the maximum length of straw. The crops of potatoes, oats, hay, and vegetables are all for use on the island by man or beast.

It is probable that very good vegetables and some fruit could be grown in sheltered spots on a larger and more intensive scale and provide needed variety to both islanders' and visitors' diets. Flowers also do well when sheltered and cared for. There would seem to be an opening for the air-freighting and selling of cut flowers.

Potatoes may still be carried home in a creel woven from the willows that are grown for the purpose in little plots about the islands. The tractors, with trailers, do a good deal of the heavier fetching and carrying of goods about the islands. Seaweed is collected, both for use as manure and for export. That exported is no longer laboriously burned in kelp kilns, but merely dried, bundled up and sent off to mainland factories, where it fetches good prices for comparatively little effort.

Fertiliser for the little fields is imported, and the potatoes are sprayed against blight with knapsack sprayers.

The Aran farmer and his wife still do a lot of daily 'travelling' to their various fields, to milk the cow, feed the calf and young stock, and carry out the various seasonal operations on the growing crops. The introduction of rain tanks to Inishmore in the 1920s reduced the amount of water-carrying very considerably. The tanks were originally only found on the big island, with its longer distances and more rapid decline in population; but they are now common on the other two, and a government grant is available for building them. They are based on the same principle as the 'dewponds' of the English downlands.

Fishing in 1972 pays better than farming, and it is the young fishermen of Inishmore who own many of the cars and motorcycles. The two smaller islands, lacking safe harbours, still work entirely with curraghs, and engage in a certain amount of small-scale fishing, including lobster fishing, quite profitably.

The main fishing fleet, however, is based on Inishmore and the harbour of Kilronan. Aran fisheries have known great success and total failure, and islanders tended to oppose Irish entry into the Common Market, whose larger vessels could easily destroy their fishing grounds.

The present revival of fishing from Inishmore began in 1960.

131

By 1971 the island was operating ten trawlers, of 50ft or so in length, and eight or nine lobster boats. The fishermen have formed a co-operative, and this, with the approval of the Minister for Local Government and Galway County Council, initiated the island's first ever housing scheme in 1971—to build fifteen houses at Kilronan. There are some sixty or seventy people involved in the fishing, and a real danger that the young men might have to look for a house on the mainland when they married, and so be lost to the islands. The Kilronan co-operative is also concerned with a generator to provide electricity, and with the possibility of developing fish-processing on the islands. At the moment the only processing is domestic drying for home use; obviously one source of new employment, including employment for women, would be for the islands to process some of their own catch instead of selling it all direct to the mainland buyers. Probably even the traditional salted and dried fish, suitably packaged, would be very attractive to visitors to the islands and for mainland shops, as it is tasty and not generally available.

THE HOME

The traditional house was all of local material bar the main roof timbers, using the local rock and island-grown thatch. There are still a number of these old houses in Aran, particularly on Inishmaan, modernised to a greater or lesser extent inside. The new houses, however, are constructed of imported materials, and look just like those on the mainland.

There is a piped water supply over most of Inishmore, and Kilronan has had some kind of a supply for a long time, but the main scheme, for the whole island, was started in 1961. In 1971 Inisheer's water scheme was still under construction, and Inishmaan's water supplies had just been surveyed. Laying pipes on the islands in some areas can be a laborious business because of the rocky terrain.

The national electricity supply had not been extended to the island by 1972. Battery-operated radios bring news and entertainment to island homes, and there are also some television sets, run off privately owned generators, and to be found in the village halls and some public houses. Apart from those who own such generators, lighting and cooking is done very often with bottled gas. Solid-fuel cookers and domestic fires burn imported coal or anthracite, and sometimes turf (peat) brought in from Connemara. The latter is by no means a cheap alternative today, as the price has risen considerably in recent years. Paraffin is also used for light and heat, and the bedroom candle is still to the fore.

The furnishing of the home approximates more and more to mainland standards and uniformity. Those who have installed their own private piped supply of water will bring it to a stainless steel kitchen sink and into a typical mainland bathroom. Galway supplies such things as building materials, household fittings and furnishings, and the goods that the islands' small shops cannot supply. No supermarkets had been opened on the islands by 1971. Imports of food now include a number of items such as bacon and creamery butter, once produced on the islands.

Island eating habits are now probably like those of the adjacent country districts of the mainland—the big plateful but not the elaborate cooking or variety of dishes. There is a lack of fresh home-grown vegetables and of fruit. Probably every home bakes a loaf of Irish soda bread for daily use. Bakers' bread is also imported, and, of course, the flour for the soda bread has to come from overseas. Home-grown potatoes and cabbage bulk largely in the menu. Fish is not eaten nearly as much as one might expect, the whole catch generally being sold abroad. But those who fish or have friends on the trawlers generally consume the miscellaneous species that belong to none of the saleable categories being boxed in bulk.

The problem of finding adequate sources of income and employment on the islands has led to many of the girls leaving for good, and to island farms being managed by elderly bachelors. The young fishermen whose intention it is to marry and settle down in their new houses at Kilronan represent a turn for the better.

133

Inishmaan has at present a number of elderly bachelors, but in 1971 there was a suggestion of a new trend in that two mainland girls were marrying into the island.

Island women tend to be home bodies, and the foundation of a branch of the Irish Countrywoman's Association (comparable to the Women's Rural Institute in Britain) on Inishmore met with little success. Even a young married woman on the islands may remark that she has enough to do, and enough interest, with home and children, without going out to meetings. In addition it is more difficult for an island ICA guild to arrange an attractive and varied programme when demonstrators and lecturers must all be transported to the islands and stay at least one night.

There are public houses on all the islands, those on Inishmore clustered at Kilronan. They are the men's club, where they enjoy the dark pints of Guinness, gossip, sing and dance. For Aranmen, like the Greeks, will dance solo or in little groups, without any women for partners. The younger island women and female visitors are beginning to edge into what used to be an exclusively male gathering in the pubs, and the stranger is, in fact, very welcome. They are a good place to meet Aranmen, especially if one understands Irish and to get the 'feel' of the islands.

The 1960s saw the construction of fine, well equipped parish halls on each of the islands, with their own electrical generators, television, regular film shows and occasional live stage performances. *Man of Aran* is shown regularly in Kilronan hall during the summer months for the benefit of visitors. There are *ceilidhs* (dances), with the music provided by islanders playing accordions and drums, and islander and visitor alike welcome to contribute a song (in any language) between the dances. Here, of course, both men and women take part, and Irish set dances are very popular. The energetic and uproarious intertwining patterns of such dances as the 'Walls of Ennis' make the crowded dance floor very much a single party having fun together. People of all ages are present, for dancing is not merely a teenage pastime, though dances take place chiefly in summer and during the

134

Christmas holidays, when the young people are at home and there are plenty of partners.

ISLAND DRESS

With increasing affluence, together with increasing contact with the outside world, Aran people are tending more and more to wear mainland fashions. No longer is wool shorn, spun and woven and then made into heavy bawneen (Irish tweed) suits. There are still a tailor or two on the islands, and it is possible to get one to make a traditional Aran suit of clothes, which has heavy tweed trousers, kept up by a coloured woven belt, and a sleeveless 'waistcoat' jacket. Some men still wear these clothes, and they are very serviceable for work on the land and at sea. So too are the rawhide pampooties, cut from untanned cowskin. Pampooties only last a matter of months and need to be kept damp to remain supple, and there are a certain number made for sale to visitors. As the hair is left outside, such shoes give a good grip on the island rocks, on which a nailed boot would slip disastrously. Traditional pampooties would, in fact, be a very good buy for a visitor spending some time on the islands and intending to do a lot of walking over the rocks, though ordinary rubber-soled plimsolls will give the same foothold.

The older women, particularly on Inishmaan, may wear the traditional full skirt of scarlet or blue cloth, and a patterned brown shawl over the head. Although originally dyes were made of local materials, in more recent times the scarlet of Connemara and Aran 'petticoats' was imported from England and is no longer manufactured. At the present time the younger generation does not seem, as in some other countries, inclined to adopt a traditional island costume for wear on special occasions. International fashions have much greater appeal, and, of course, are today much easier and cheaper to purchase.

A number of Aran women still knit, and they make a certain amount of 'pin money' by so doing. The Aran island knitted patterns are now being produced all over Ireland and even outside that country. They are complicated designs of knots and cables, which show up best on white bawneen wool. It is said that a drowned body was identified even though badly battered, by the womenfolk recognising the gansey they had knitted.

In Aran the children learn these patterns from their parents, and they are knitted to the traditional designs without any written set of directions. A number of Aran women also crochet, sometimes following their own designs and colour schemes.

The cris is a very colourful and attractive woven belt, whose pattern is established in the long threads of the warp, which may be stretched out between any two handy objects, such as two chairs, to set up the required length. The woof is then woven in, the finished end being held in the hand. A cris intended for hard wear, such as holding up trousers, is made from double knitting wool, but one intended simply for decorative use is made from a lighter weight wool. The Aran cris, like the Aran sweater and cardigan, has become high fashion wear, and the majority of those on sale in Irish shops are made on the mainland, not in the islands.

There is no very great profit in such knitting and weaving at home when the price of wool, plus postage, and the time required to complete each article is counted in. For instance, one elderly knitter in Inishmore received only £7 for an Aran gansey that had taken a fortnight to make and needed £2 worth of wool (including carriage from the mainland).

THE LAW, MEDICINE AND EDUCATION

Three Guards (police) are based at Kilronan on Inishmore, and they visit the other two islands when necessary. Police work on the Aran Islands is largely concerned with a multitude of routine duties rather than criminal investigations. Until a few years ago the Guards recorded the rainfall at Kilronan. The two smaller islands seem able to maintain their own good order quite successfully.

Each island has a resident nurse. The present doctor (1972) is married to one of the Guards and lives at Kilronan on Inishmore. The Aran medical service is based on the intention of foreseeing any emergency and transporting patients to the mainland before their condition becomes serious. Babies are normally born in mainland maternity hospitals. If there is an emergency case, the lifeboat acts as the hospital boat. The patient from the smaller islands may still have to make a tough journey overseas, first by curragh and then by lifeboat. The aeroplane is, of course, a new factor in the situation and was already transporting patients from Inishmore in 1970. In the first year of its operation one patient was flown out from Killeany by the light from car headlamps, and made a successful recovery in a mainland hospital.

The lifeboat itself is also based at Kilronan. The islands got their first lifeboat, which was the old one from Rosslare, in 1927 —an open boat with an 80hp engine. The 'roll of honour' of the islands' lifeboat and its crew—a long list of ships helped and sick people taken off the islands—is listed on a plaque at Kilronan harbour.

Education begins on the islands, in the Irish language. There is one primary school on each of the smaller islands but Inishmore requires several to cover its greater size. Inishmore also has a vocational school, which, in addition to the ordinary range of subjects, runs a course in marine engineering for boys who are intending to become fishermen.

Ordinary secondary schooling must take place on the mainland, and, as this is now free to all children, there is a complete exodus of the islands' teenage youngsters. The mainland boarding schools to which they go are Irish-speaking, but the fact that they go at all is quite a new factor in their upbringing. General free secondary education is very new in Ireland and its effects on the islands have yet to be seen. A number of island children have, of course, attended mainland secondary schools and possibly gone on to university, but only now is the opportunity made available to all. There is a danger of breaking the young people's ties with their island homes very effectively. Even as it is, few islanders with such mainland education seem to wish to try and make some sort of career for themselves in Aran. To a certain extent this, of course, merely reflects the lack of suitable openings there.

Irish remains the first language of the islands, and it is so universal that it is hard to realise that there was once some danger of its loss. Inisheer, in particular, seems to have once been in danger of becoming anglicised. The Gaelic League, founded in 1893 and active in the islands, was one organisation that helped encourage enthusiasm for and the use of the old tongue.

The islands do not appear to have produced any notable writers in Irish recently. Liam O'Flaherty, the novelist, was born on Inishmore in 1896, but his genius is cosmopolitan and expressed in English. The now deserted Blaskets in county Kerry, however, had several native writers, who left vivid descriptions in Irish of their island life.

Most islanders are bilingual and have excellent English, so the visitor is not likely to encounter any real 'language barrier'. But it must be said that Aran people are most fully themselves, almost different people, when they are expressing their thoughts in their own language. The visitor with some knowledge of Irish will be able to understand Aran people and get to know them far better than one with only English. The placenames of the islands are also Irish, and, as with Gaelic placenames everywhere, in both Ireland and Scotland, are of great interest and often highly descriptive of the places to which they relate. Some of the names on the Ordnance Survey map appear in rather strange phonetic anglicised spellings—the best the original surveyors could do, but confusing to the person today who is trying to spell out their original Irish form and meaning. A list of some of the more interesting place-names of the islands forms Appendix E.

In 1972 Radio Telefís Eireann, the Irish broadcasting and television organisation, set up a Gaeltacht radio station whose transmissions are wholly in Irish. For Aran, as well as for other Irish-speaking (Gaeltacht) districts, this represents a much needed service, and a means of keeping the language in full use in Irish broadcasting. Up to the foundation of the new station, the Irish language was used in only a few of the daily radio programmes and even less frequently on television. As radio and television enter into nearly everyone's daily life, this barrage of English adds to the continual attrition a language like Irish is undergoing. It tends to improve the listeners' and viewers' English to the detriment of their Irish.

THE CHURCH

The Aran Islanders are Roman Catholics and their whole religious and moral outlook is structured and directed by their deeply held faith. Even the passing greetings on the road are, in their traditional Irish forms, blessings.

As with schools, so with churches : one each on the two smaller islands, and three along the length of Inishmore. The parish priest and one curate live at Kilronan. The second curate lives on Inisheer, where on Sunday he celebrates one mass, and then crosses to Inishmaan by curragh to celebrate a second. The island's curragh-owners take it in turns to bring him across, and, of course, it can be a rough ride, even with an outboard motor to push the craft along. Inishmaan people watch the sea and pick out the black speck as it appears and disappears among the wave-crests, and then some of the men go down to the pier to meet him, while the rest of the island begins to move toward the church.

Even with the relaxed fasting laws of the Catholic Church today, these two Sunday masses represent quite a hard morning's work, and in the old days when the priest could not break his fast from midnight until after the last mass was said, it must often have been an ordeal. Synge told a story of one such Sunday morning. He was lying fed and warm in the sunshine when he was greeted by the curate, who was wet, hungry and tired. 'Tell

139

me', said the priest, 'did you read your Bible this morning?' Synge said he had not. 'Well, begob, Mr Synge, if you ever go to Heaven, you'll have a great laugh at us.'

The Latin of the mass has now been replaced by Irish, and the congregation, which still follows the old custom of the men sitting on the right and women on the left, joins vigorously in the responses. A small choir sings in Irish at the entry, offertory, communion and conclusion. As the people go up to communion, the choir may sing 'Cead mile failte rot, a Iosa' (A hundred thousand welcomes, Jesus). Here, at least, the vernacular liturgy has been welcomed; the mass is more fully understood and there is a certain proud satisfaction for this island people in praying in their own native language.

The Church of Ireland (Anglican) building at Kilronan is now a roofless shell; it and its parson served the small community of 'Protestants' (which in Ireland covers both Anglican and non-episcopal denominations) once living on the islands—police, coast-guards and a few others. These Protestants, who were mostly not islanders, have long since gone. The heyday of the little parish belonged to a period of sharp division between the Churches and often of bitter controversy and proselytising. A more ecumenical spirit is now found between the Churches in the Irish Republic, and it was to the Roman Catholic priest that the Church of Ireland addressed some tentative queries in 1971 about organising Sunday services for the many non-Catholic visitors to the islands in summertime. When the scheme materialised the following year, it was with the help and co-operation of the Catholic Church.

TOURISM AND THE ISLANDS' FUTURE

Tourism now bulks large in island life. Visitors come from all over the world, as well as from the rest of Ireland. There are on Inishmore a number of regular guest houses, as well as houses that take in a few visitors; on the other islands most of the houses take in visitors or children coming to improve their Irish. Only one of the guest houses, at Kilronan, stays open all the year round.

There are, as yet, no large hotels. Some visitors bring their own tents and camp.

In small islands with little other major industry, this massive influx of visitors can be both an economic blessing and a cultural menace. There is always the danger of 'putting on an act' for the stranger, as well as living too much for the exploitation of tourism.

The visitors are a major source of income, to the houses in which they stay, to the men who take them sightseeing in pony and trap, and to the boatmen, if they go sea angling or curragh-sailing. The other major sources of income are the presently prosperous fishing and the sale of cattle. The fishing will continue to do well as long as the local waters are not over-fished nor invaded by larger and better equipped ships from Common Market countries.

Government money helps the islanders by way of public assistance payments, old-age pensions, and various grants in aid. Islanders working elsewhere send contributions home. There is need for more diversification to bring not only more money but more opportunities for island youngsters to remain on the islands if they so wish. Fish-processing could be one such outlet, and perhaps the better organisation of the making of souvenirs and their selling. Currently, the pierhead souvenir shop at Kilronan is run by a mainland firm, and not all its 'Aran' knitwear or crises are made on the the islands. It would be better if there was a shop selling only Aran-made products—knitwear, woven garments, pampooties, and perhaps fish dried in the traditional manner. Pampooties as presently made are not suitable for use indoors, since the uncured skin will both harden and smell. If they were of skin cured, but with the hair left on, they would be a most attractive 'buy' to use around the house as a soft slipper. The trial production of tulip bulbs on Inishmaan was successful, and the intensive production of both flowers and vegetables could obviously be undertaken in the small island fields where the soil is suitable. More soft fruit and vegetables would be a useful addition to the menu in the guest houses as well as for the islanders themselves.

Some people rent island cottages for summer visits, and this idea, common on the mainland, might well be extended. On the mainland houses have been built with traditional exteriors but with modern amenities; renting them for a holiday makes a pleasant change from staying in a hotel or guest house, and Aran might consider this prospect.

It remains true that living on offshore islands like Aran at the present time presents many problems and difficulties unknown to the mainlander. The prosperity of such island communities is not an impossibility but it needs much hard effort, thought, and, necessarily, continued aid from government funds to get new developments on their feet.

Page 143 Crafts:
(right) thatching

(left) making
criosanna (belts) is
still a common craft,
practised by men
and women

Page 144 1970 communications: *(left)* yacht tying up at Kilronan harbour. Visitors come to the islands from all over the world, many yachtsmen among them; *(below)* the *Islander* aircraft which inaugurated the islands' air services in 1970 brings the daily newspapers

APPENDIX A

EXPLORING THE ISLANDS

It is possible to ship a car out to Kilronan on the deck of the *Naomh Eanna* but it is hardly worth the trouble and expense. A motorcycle or ordinary bicycle would, however, be useful on Inishmore, though bicycles may be hired, as well as a taxi or a pony and trap; but on all the islands exploration is best done on foot.

The map to use is the $\frac{1}{2}$in Ordnance Survey, sheet 14. This shows also the whole of Galway Bay and the adjacent coasts of counties Galway and Clare, including the limestone *karst* country of the Burren.

On the islands the Irish Tourist Board have erected maps at the landing places showing the location of the principal monuments, as well as signposting them and fixing small informative plaques in English and Irish at the actual sites.

Rubber-soled shoes or, in the rougher parts, even boots should be worn, as the limestone pavements need footwear that gives a good grip. Nailed soles merely skid off such rock.

It is advisable to use the existing *boreens* (lanes) and field gaps as far as possible when travelling cross-country. But be careful when climbing some of the stone walls, and you will certainly have to climb them, for they may be precariously poised. Not only may you hurt yourself, but you may also let the sheep into the oats through the resulting gap.

One may walk right round the two smaller islands along the high-tide mark and the storm beaches. On Inishmore the exploration of the coast involves a much greater distance and is best taken in stages. Obviously one should go along at least part of

I

145

the great cliffs of Inishmore at Doocaher or Dun Aengus, and see how they fall sheer to the sea below.

There is one very attractive walk from Kilronan out towards Killeany, and then by an old road (which the islanders call the 'new road') along the 'back' of Inishmore to Ourtnagapple, from which one emerges once again on to the main island road near Kilmurvey. This old road is untarred, with bare rock forming its surface here and there and stone walls on either side. It does not visit any important monuments, but each field is full of wild-flowers, and there are vast views back over Inishmore, to the Burren in Clare and to the Twelve Bens in Connemara in county Galway.

On Inishmaan there is a pleasant round to be made by following a boreen that passes Dun Moher and heads down to the western shore. Here, very finely developed, are the wave-cut limestone terraces above normal high tides, in which the puffing holes occur. Back of them, equally well developed, is the immense storm beach of tumbled boulders. By following this northwards one finally arrives at Gregory's Sound, and the cairn of stones called Synge's Chair that overlooks it. Thence, a very narrow path between high walls leads back to the main cluster of houses under Dun Conor.

On Inisheer there is an enjoyable stroll from the village down to the lighthouse, with a deviation to the shore to visit the wreck of the *Plassy* rusting on her perch on the storm-beach rocks.

PRINCIPAL MONUMENTS

INISHMORE

Megalithic tomb:
  Above Teampall an Cheathrair Aluinn at Cowrugh

Stone 'forts':
  Dun Aengus
  Dun Oghil
  Dun Onaght
  Doocaher (Dubh Cathair)—headland fort

Old churches and monastic sites:
  'Seven Churches', Onaght
  Teampall MacDuagh and Teampall na Naomh at Kilmurvey
  Teampall an Cheathrair Aluinn
  Teampall Assurnidhe
  Monaster Kieran
  Killeany, including Teampall Benan on ridge above and stump
    of high cross

High cross fragments:
  Killeany
  'Seven Churches', Onaght

Early inscribed pillars with crosses/inscriptions:
  'Seven Churches', Onaght
  Monaster Kieran
  Killeany

APPENDIX B

Later castles:

Arkyn, Killeany

Other ruins:

Old lighthouse at Oghil

Beehive drystone huts (cloghanes/clochans):

Clochan na Carraige in Kilmurvey townland. (Off main road from Kilmurvey to Onaght). Others, in various stages of ruin, occur at many places in the three islands

INISHMAAN

Megalithic tomb:

Dermot and Grania's bed below Dun Moher

Stone 'forts':

Dun Conor
Dun Moher

Old churches and monastic sites:

Kilcananagh
Teampall Seacht Mic Righ near present parish church—with cross on saint's grave

INISHEER

Ancient burial ground, etc (Bronze Age):

Knockgrannia (Cnoc Raithnighe)

Stone 'forts':

Rath at O'Briens' castle

Old churches and monastic sites:

Teampall Chaomhain.
Kilgobnet
Creggankeel 'fort'—Cill na Seacht n-Inion

148

Later castles:

O'Briens' castle (Furmina Castle)

Other remains:

Eighteenth-century signal tower on ridge of island

APPENDIX C

FLORA

It may be useful to list the Aran plants given by R. Lloyd Praegar in *The Botanist in Ireland* (1934).

Very Abundant or Abundant
  Adiantum. Maidenhair fern
  Arenaris verna. Spring sandwort
  Asperula cynanchica. Squinancywort
  Carlina. Carline thistle
  Ceterach. Rustyback
  Cornua sanguinea. Dogwood
  Euphrasia salisburgensis. Eyebright
  Galium boreale. Northern bedstraw
  Galium sylvestre. Heath bedstraw
  Gentiana verna. Spring gentian
  Geranium sanguineum. Bloody cranesbill
  Helianthemum canum. Hoary rockrose
  Pimpinella major. Greater burnet
  Rubia peregrina. Wild madder
  Sesleria. Bluegrass
  Spiranthes spiralis. Common lady's tresses
  Viola hirta. Hairy violet

Less widely Distributed
  Allium Babingtonii. Garlic
  Arabis Brownii. Rockcress
  Blackstonia Yellow-wort
  Calamintha ascendea. Calamint

150

Carduus nutans. Musk thistle
Chenopodium rubrum. Red goosefoot
Crambe. Seakale
Cuscuta trifolii. Lesser Dodder var
Equisetum variegatum. Variegated horsetail
Erodium moschatum. Musk storksbill
Juncus macer. Mace reed
Juncus subnodulosus
Juniperus communis. Juniper
Ophrys apifera. Bee orchid
Orobanche hederae. Lesser Broomrape var
Orobanche rubra. Red broomrape
Rhamnus catharticus. Buckthorn
Sagina subulata. Pearlwort
Saxifraga hirta
Sedum anglicum. English stonecrop
Sedum roseum. Roseroot

Rare Species
  Ajuga pyramidalis. Erect bugle
  Astragalus danicus. Purple milkwort (only Irish station)
  Calamagrostis epigeios. Bushgrass
  Saxifraga Sternbergii

Indigenous Trees and Shrubs
  Blackthorn
  Common Buckthorn
  Dogwood
  Guelder Rose
  Hawthorn
  Hazel
  Juniper
  Oak
  Spindle

APPENDIX D

POPULATION FIGURES

Year	Inisheer	Inishmaan	Inishmore	Total
1812				2,400
1821	421	387	2,285	3,093
1831				3,191
1841	456	473	2,592	3,521
1851	518	503	2,312	3,333
1861	532	478	2,289	3,299
1871	495	433	2,122	3,050
1881	497	473	2,193	3,163
1891	455	456	1,996	2,907
1901	483	421	1,959	2,863
1911	480	420	1,779	2,679
1926	409	380	1,368	2,157
1936	445	375	1,289	2,109
1946	447	388	1,136	1,971
1951	388	361	1,019	1,768
1956	376	361	944	1,681
1961	358	357	933	1,648
1966	345	342	925	1,612
1971	313	319	864	1,496

APPENDIX E

PLACENAMES

The name *Aran* itself is usually said to be derived from *aru*, genitive *arann* meaning a kidney. It is possible to see a kidney shape in the outline of Inishmore. *Aran* is the Irish for bread, but this does not seem to have any bearing on the islands' name. Aran is variously spelt with one or two rs, and of course there is another Aran in Ireland, in Donegal, and one among the Scottish islands. The philologist W. J. Watson claimed that the Scottish Arran had a different derivation from the Irish one, and thought that it could be a pre-Celtic word. Its meaning was unknown but he compared it with other 'Aran' placenames in Wales, which could have the same origin.

The following list includes the principal placenames in the Aran Islands, listed by their anglicised spellings, with the Irish original following. It should be noted that there may be one or more spellings, which are all acceptable—for example, Inisheer and Inishere.

Grateful acknowledgment is made for assistance with some of the placenames from Eamonn de hOir of the Irish placenames commission.

Amurvy, Lough. Loch an Mhuirbhigh. Lake of the sea plain or sandy plain.
Ballinlisheen. Baile an Lisin. Hamlet of the small earthen ring fort. *Baile* anglicised *Bally* is very common in Irish placenames —it means a township in the Scottish or Irish sense, a small group of houses. *Lis* is one of the several words for a ring fort;

153

it is mostly used of earthen forts and occurs in names like *Lismore*, big fort.

Brannock Islands. Oilean da Bhranog. Island of the two little ravens, or of Dobhranog, which might be a diminutive of the name Branog and mean a little raven. It could be a saint's name.

Bungowla. Bun Gabhla. Bottom of the fork.

Doocaher. Dubh Cathair. The Black Fort. *Cathair* is another name for a ring fort, usually a large and extensive one. It is often translated 'city', in the sense that a great monastery in its enclosure could be called a monastic 'city'.

Dun Aengus. Dun Aenghus. Aengus' Fort. *Dun* is the usual name for a large fortified rath or ring fort, often of stone.

Dun Conor/Doon Conor. Dun Conchobhair. Conor's Fort. *Doon* is another anglicised spelling of *dun*.

Dun Oghil, Dun Onaght. See Oghil and Onaght below. Forts of Oghil and Onaght.

Cora Point. Gob na Cora. Probably 'point of the stepping stones', but the meaning of *cora* is doubtful in this context.

Cowrugh. Corruch. Probably means the 'uneven sea inlet' but might also be a corruption of Caradoc, a saint's name.

Eararna. Iarairne. In this context *iar* may not mean 'west' but 'back of'. *Airne* might refer to the name of the islands as a whole, Aran. 'Back of the island'.

Fardurris Point. Fardoras, a lintel.

Furmina (O'Briens' Castle and district on Inisheer). Formna, a ridge.

Glassan Rock. Aill na nGlasog, cliff of the *glasoga*, a species of fish caught there.

Illaunatee or Straw Island. Oilean na Tui. Island of the straw or thatch. Here much rye was once grown for island roofing.

Inisheer (or Inishere). Inis Oirr. The eastern island. Derived from the older form *Inis Oirthir*. *Inis Thiar*, another variant is neither correct Irish or current pronunciation and would indicate, wrongly, that the island lay to the west, not the east, of the group.

Inishmaan. Inis Meain. Middle Island.

Inishmore. Inis Mor. Big Island.

Kilcananagh (also known as Temple Kenanagh). Cill Chean-
nannach. *Cill* is a very common Irish word for a church or
chapel, and appears in placenames as *Kil* followed by the name
of the saint who founded the church, or the person to whom it
is dedicated. Kilcananagh may mean the Church of the Canons,
but it could refer to a saint called Kenanagh, who is locally
identified with the Gregory of Gregory's Sound.

Killeany. Cill Einne. St Enda's church.

Kill na Seacht Inghean. Cill na Seacht n-Inion. The Church of the
Seven Daughters.

Kilmurvey. Cill Mhuirbhigh. Church of the sea plain or sandy
plain.

Kilronan. Cill Ronain. St Ronan's church.

Leaba Brecain. Leaba Bhreacain. St Brecan's 'bed'. The word
leaba, usually translated *bed* is very commonly used for the
grave of a saint.

Lough Atalia. Loch an tSaile. Lake of the brine.

Lough More. Loch Mor. The great or big lake.

Lough Oorgowla. Probably Loch Bhun Gabhla, Bungowla lake,
and should be more correctly anglicised as Bungowla (qv) and
not Oorgowla.

Moher or Moor. An Mothar. The word has various meanings—
thicket or grove or ruin; in county Clare it is said to be used
of a field.

Monaster Kieran. Monaster Ciaran. St Ciaran's monastery. This
saint is the Ciaran who founded the great monastery of Clonmacnois on the River Shannon near Athlone in AD 545, also
known as the Connacht monastery. Aran people usually just
speak of 'Monaster'.

Oghil. Eochaill. Yew wood. Present Irish scholarship is convinced
that this does mean yew wood, though O'Donovan of the
Ordnance Survey Letters (1839) doubted it. Dun Oghil is Dun
Eochaill, Fort of the Yew Wood.

Onaght. Eoghanacht. This is the name of an Irish sept or clan.

Dun Eoghanachta (Dun Onaght) is the fort of the Eoghanacht clan.

Ourtnagapple. Now generally spelled Gort na gCapall, field of the horses. But the placenames commission has recorded that the pronunciation is really Urt na gCapall, with the meaning of Urt in doubt.

Portmurry. Mis-spelling for Portmurvey, Port Mhuirbhigh, port of the sandy or sea plain

Sruffaun. Sruthan. Streamlet.

Teampall Chaomhain. St Caomhen's (Cavan's) Church. Marked on the maps also as St Cavan's Church.

Teglach Enda. Teachlach Einne. St Enda's house, spelt on the 1in Ordnance map, Tighlagheany.

Templeancheathrairaluinn. Teampall an Cheathrair Aluinn. The church of the Four Comely Saints, or, as often translated, of the Four Beauties. The holy well by the church is Bollan an Cheathrair Aluinn.

Templeaphoyle. Teampall an Phoill. Probably 'church of the hollow'.

Temple Benan. Teampall Beanan. St Benan's church. Teampall, derived from the Latin for a temple, is a common Irish word for a church.

Templebrecan. Teampall Bhreacain. St Brecan's church

Templemacduagh. Teampall Mac Duach. St MacDuach's church.

Templemurry. Teampall Muire. Mary's Church (the Blessed Virgin).

Templenaneeve. Teampall na Naomh. Church of the saint.

Temple Saght Macree. Teampall na Seacht mac Righ. Church of the Seven Princes (ie sons of kings).

Templesoorney. Teampall Assurnaidhe. Church of St Soorney

Tobar Einne. St Enda's well. Tobar is the usual name for a well or spring and occurs in many Irish placenames.

Trawkeera. Tra Caorach. Strand of the sheep.

Wirrabee Lough. Loch an Mhuirbhigh. Lake of sea plain or sandy plain. Loughamurvy is suggested as a better anglicisation of this name.

RODERICK O'FLAHERTY'S DESCRIPTION IN 1684

'The Three Isles of Aran half Barony extending in length from east to west, have the Barony of Moycullen on the north, Moyclea in Corcomroe Barony and county of Clare on the east, and the cape of Kerry Head far off in sight stretched out in the sea on the south. They are fenced on the south side with very high cliffs, some three score, some four score, and five score fathom deep against the western ocean's approach.

'The soil is almost paved over with stones, so as in some places nothing is to be seen but large stones with wide openings between them where cattle break their legs. Scarce any other stones there but lime stones and marble fit for tombstones, chimney mantle trees and high crosses. Among these stones is very sweet pasture, so that beef and mutton are better and earlier in season here than elsewhere and of late there is plenty of cheese and tillage mucking and corn is the same with the seaside tract. In some places, the plow goes.

'On the shore grows samphire in plenty, ringroot or sea holly, and sea cabbage. Here are Cornish choughs with red legs and bills. Here are ayries of hawks and birds, which never fly save over the sea and therefore are used to be eaten on fasting days, to catch which people go down with ropes tied about them, into the caves of cliffs in the night and with a candle light kill abundance of them. Here are several wells and pools; yet in extraordinary dry weather, people must turn their cattle out of the islands and the corn fails. They have no fuel but cow dung dried with the sun, unless they bring turf in from the western continent.

'They have cloghans, a kind of building of stones laid one upon the other which are brought to a roof without any manner of mortar to cement them, some of which cabins will hold forty men on their floor; so ancient that nobody knows how long ago any of them was made. Scarcity of wood and store of fit stones, without peradventure, found out the first invention.

'There is a west island on the south [*recte* north] west, called Ilan na [Da] Branoge, where they go to slaughter seals yearly and where there is abundance of samphire.

'From the Isles of Aran and the west continent, often appears visible that uncharted island called O'Brasil and in Irish, Beg Ara, or the Lesser Aran, set down in charts of navigation, whether it be real and firm land kept hidden by the special ordinance of God or the terrestrial paradise, or else some illusion of airy clouds appearing on the surface of the sea, or the craft of evil spirits, is more than our judgements can sound out.

'The islands of Aran for the numerous multitude of Saints there living of old and interred or there trained in religious austerity and propagating monastic discipline in other parts, are venerable for many sacred churches, chapells, wells, crosses and sepulchres, and other holy reliques of saints still there extant as monuments of their piety; reverenced for many rare privileges of sacred places therein and the instant divine punishments inflicted on such as dare violate or prophane; frequently visited by Christians in pilgrimage for devotion, acts of penance and miraculous virtues there wrought.

'Ara Mhor, the greatest and furthest west of these contains twenty four quarters of land and is twenty four miles in compass, whereon, on the south side stands Dun Engus, a large fortified place on the brim of a high cliff a hundred fathoms deep, being a great wall of bare stones without any mortar, in compass as big as a large castle bawn, with several long stones on the outside erected slopewise against any assaults. It is named of Engus Mac Uathmore of the reliques of the Bolgmen in Ireland, there living about the birth time of Christ. On the east side thereof, the island is so low that about the year 1640 upon an extraordinary inundation, the sea overflowing that bank, went across the island to the north-west.

'The King's Castle and manor of Arkin stood on the north side over the ship harbour, for the service of which castle, all the patents in capite of West Connacht, granted by Queen Elizabeth and King James were held, in place whereof now stands a citadel, in the usurper Cromwell's time erected.'

From Roderick O'Flaherty's *Chorographical Description of West Connacht*, written for the information of Sir William Petty in 1684.

BIBLIOGRAPHY

AALEN, F. H. A. 'The Evolution of the Traditional House in Western Ireland', *Journal Royal Society of Antiquaries of Ireland*, vol 96, part 1 (1966) 47–58

ARMSTRONG, EDWARD. A. 'Birds of the Aran Islands', *Irish Naturalist's Journal*, vol 12, no 8 (October, 1957), 207–8

BARRETT, JOHN H. 'Birds seen on Inishmore, Aran Islands, 6–9 November 1957', *Irish Naturalist's Journal*, vol 12, no 12 (October, 1958), 314–16

BURKE, OLIVER J. *The South Isles of Aran* (London, 1887)

Burren. Short guide by various authors—of interest in that it is a part of the same limestone area as Aran (Limerick, 1971)

COLGAN, NATHANIEL. 'Witchcraft in the Aran Islands', *Journal Royal Society of Antiquaries of Ireland*, vol 25 (1895), 84–85

COLGAN, NATHANIEL. 'Notes on the Flora of the Aran Islands', *Irish Naturalist's Journal* (1893), 75–8, 106–11

CORKERY, DANIEL. *The Fortunes of the Irish Language* (Dublin, 1954)

DANAHER, KEVIN. *Folktales of the Irish Countryside* (Cork, 1970)

DE PAOR, LIAM. 'The Limestone Crosses of Clare and Aran', *Journal of the Galway Archaeological and Historical Society*, vol 26 (1955–6), 53–71

DUIGNAN, MICHAEL V. AND KILLANIN, LORD. *The Shell Guide to Ireland*, 2nd edition (1969)

FREEMAN, T. W. *Ireland. Its Physical, Historical, Social and Economic Geography* (London, 1950)

GAILEY, R. A. 'Settlement and Population in the Aran Islands'. *Irish Geography*, vol 4, no 1 (1959), 65–78

GAILEY, R. A. 'Aspects of Change in a Rural Community', *Ulster Folklife*, vol 5 (1959), 27–34

K
161

BIBLIOGRAPHY

GOULDEN, J. R. W. 'Arkin : Outpost in Aran', *Irish Sword,* vol 1, no 4 (1952–3), 262–7

HACKETT, EARLE AND FOLAN, M. E. 'The ABO and RH Blood Groups of the Aran Islanders', *Irish Journal of Medical Science* (June, 1958), 247–61

HARBISON, PETER. *Guide to the National Monuments of Ireland* (Dublin, 1970)

HARDIMAN, JAMES. *The History of the Town and County of the Town of Galway* (Dublin, 1820)

HART, H. C. *A list of Plants found in the Islands of Aran, Galway Bay* (Dublin, 1875)

HEDDERMAN, B. N. *Glimpses of My Life in Aran* (Bristol, 1917)

HENRY, F. *Irish Art* (1940)

HENRY, F. *Early Christian Irish Art* (Dublin, 1954)

HORNELL, JAMES. *British Coracles and Irish Curraghs* (1938)

HOOTON, ERNEST A. AND DUPERTUIS, C. WESLEY. *The Physical Anthropology of Ireland* (Cambridge, Mass, 1955)

KAVANAGH, MARY. *A Bibliography of the County Galway* (Galway, 1965)

KILBRIDE, WILLIAM. 'Notes of some Antiquities on Aranmore in the Bay of Galway', *Journal of the Historical and Archaeological Association of Ireland,* vol 1, 3rd series (1868–69), part 1 (1868), 102–18

KINAHAN, GEORGE HENRY. 'Notes on some of the ancient villages in the Aran Isles, county of Galway', *Proceedings Royal Irish Academy,* vol 10 (1866–70), 25

KINAHAN, G. H., LEONARD, H. AND CRUISE, R. J. *Memoirs of the Geological Survey of Ireland* (1871), Sheets 104 and 113

KLIMM, L. E. 'Inishmore : an outpost island', *Geographical Review,* vol 17 (1927), 387–96.

KLIMM, L. E. 'The Relation between field patterns and jointing in the Aran islands', *Geographical Review* vol 25 (1935), 618–24

KLIMM, L. E. 'The Rain Tanks of Aran', *Bulletin of the Geographical Society of Philadelphia* (1936), 73–84

LEASK, H. G. 'Finding of Whales' Vertebrae in Clochan-na-Carraige, Inishmore, Aran, Co. Galway', *Journal Royal Society of Antiquaries of Ireland,* vol 73 (1943), 24

162

LEWIS, SAMUEL. *A Topographical Dictionary of Ireland* (1837)

LIONARD, PADRAIG. 'Early *Irish* Grave Slabs', *Proceedings Royal Irish Academy*, vol 61 C (1960–61), 95–169

MACALISTER, R. A. S. In *Journal of the Royal Society of Antiquaries of Ireland* :
'Crosses at Kilbrecan, Aran', vol 25 (1895), 379–80
'The Stone of the Seven Romans' Series 6, vol 3 (1913), 344
'The Cross Inscribed Holed Stone at Mainster Chiarain, Aran, Co. Galway', vol 52 (1922), 177

McNEILL, D. B. *Irish Passenger Steamship Services*, vol 2 (Newton Abbot, 1971)

MASON, T. H. 'The Antiquarian Remains of Inisheer, Aran, county Galway', *Journal Royal Society of Antiquaries of Ireland*, vol 68 (1938), 196–200

MASON, T. H. *The Islands of Ireland* (1936)

MESSENGER, JOHN C. *Inis Beag. Isle of Ireland* (New York, 1969)

MOULD, D. D. C. POCHIN. *Irish Pilgrimage* (an account of the ancient Irish pilgrimages) (Dublin, 1955)

MOULD, D. D. C. POCHIN. *The Irish Saints* (critical biographies) (Dublin, 1964)

MULLEN, PATRICK. *Man of Aran* (1934)

MURPHY, DENIS. 'On two sepulchral urns found in June 1885, in the South Isles of Arran', *Proceedings of the Royal Irish Academy*, vol 12 (1879–88), 476–9

MURPHY, GERARD. *The Ossianic Lore and Romantic Tales of Medieval Ireland* (Dublin, 1955)

O'BRIEN, DONOUGH. *History of the O'Briens* (1949)

O'BRIEN, T. V. *History of the Aran Islands (Inismore, Inismeadhon and Inisiar) county Galway, Eire. From the 13th to the 20th centuries, drawn from contemporary sources* (July, 1945). MS 3198 in library of Trinity College Dublin

O'DONOVAN, JOHN. *Ordnance Survey Letters* (Galway, 1839)

O'FLAHERTY, T. *Aranmen All* (Dublin, 1934)

O'KELLY, MICHAEL J. 'Problems of Irish Ring Forts', *The Irish Sea Province in Archaeology and History*, Cambrian Archaeological Association (1970), 50–54

O'LANNDAIGH, ART. Account (in Irish) of seeing Hy Brasil in G. A.

BIBLIOGRAPHY

Little. *Brendan the Navigator* (Dublin, 1945), 196. This book also contains drawings of the various maps showing Hy Brasil and Brendan's Island.

O'NEILL HENCKEN, H. *Cahercommaun. A Stone Fort in County Clare.* Special volume, Royal Society Antiquaries of Ireland (Dublin, 1938)

O'RAHILLY, T. F. *Early Irish History and Mythology* (Dublin, 1946)

O'RIORDAIN, SEAN P. *Antiquities of the Irish Countryside* (1942)

O'SIOCHAIN, P. A. *Aran. Islands of Legend* (Dublin)

PHILLIPS, R. A. 'The Non-Marine Mollusca of Inishmore', *Irish Naturalist's Journal,* vol 19 (1910), 115–18

PRAEGAR, ROBERT LLOYD. *The Botanist in Ireland* (Dublin, 1934)

PRAEGAR, ROBERT LLOYD. *Natural History of Ireland. A sketch of its flora and fauna* (1950)

RUTLEDGE, R. F. 'A List of the Birds of the Counties Galway and Mayo', *Proceedings Royal Irish Academy,* 52, B8 (1950), 315–81

RUTLEDGE, R. F. *Ireland's Birds. Their Distribution and Migrations* (1966)

SKELTON, ROBIN. *J. M. Synge and His World* (1971)

STELFOX, A. W. 'On the Occurrence of a Peculiar Race of the Humble Bee, Bombus Smithianus White, on the Aran Islands in Western Ireland', *Irish Naturalist's Journal,* vol 4, no 12 (November, 1933), 235–8

SYNGE, J. M. *The Aran Islands* (1907, but there are several recent reprintings)

THOMPSON, WILLIAM. *The Natural History of Ireland,* 4 vols (1849–56)

WESTROPP, THOMAS JOHNSON. 'A Study of the Fort of Dun Aenghusa in Inishmore, Aran Islands, Galway Bay : its Plan, Growth and Records', *Proceedings of the Royal Irish Academy,* vol 28 (1909–10), 1–46. Reprinted as a separate volume (Dublin, 1910)

WESTROPP, THOMAS JOHNSON. 'A Study of the Early Forts and Stone Huts in Inishmore, Aran Isles, Galway Bay', *Proceedings of the Royal Irish Academy,* vol 28 (1909–10), 174–200
Westropp's paper on the antiquities of the Aran islands, first published in the *Journal of the Royal Society of Antiquaries of Ireland* (vol 25, 1895, 250–78) was reprinted by the society in its *Illustrated Guide to the Northern, Western and Southern*

Islands, and Coast of Ireland (Dublin, 1905) and again, with additional material by the Mount Salus Press in *The Aran Islands* (Dublin, 1971)

WESTROPP, THOMAS JOHNSON. 'Brasil and the Legendary Islands of the North Atlantic', *Proceedings Royal Irish Academy*, vol 30 C (1912–13), 223–60

WILSON, T. G. *The Irish Lighthouse Service* (Dublin, 1968)

ACKNOWLEDGEMENTS

I wish to thank first of all the people of the Aran Islands for their help and hospitality on my various visits. Nor must the continued friendly assistance of Aer Arann in all my recent flights to the islands be forgotten.

Thanks are due, too, to the National Library of Ireland, Dublin, for permission to reproduce one of the photographs from the Laurence Collection; and to Bord Failte Eireann and the *Irish Times*, both of whom allowed me to examine their extensive collections of Aran photographs and select some of them for use in this book. Bord Failte's pictures of an old style family group round the fire (p. 54) and of Islanders in traditional dress, small boys in petticoats, waiting on the *Dun Aengus* (p. 71) are an important witness to island life as it was not so long ago, and in contrast to my own sets of photographs, most of which were taken in 1971.

INDEX

INDEX